Head Games

De-Colonizing the Psychotherapeutic Process

Nikitah Okembe-RA Imani

UNIVERSITY PRESS OF AMERICA,® INC.
Lanham • Boulder • New York • Toronto • Plymouth, UK

This volume is dedicated to the ancient and near African spirits and to the great African people in the physical worldwide. It is further dedicated to God and to the Lord Jesus Christ, the Afrikan messiah of all mankind. It is dedicated to my parents, Mr. and Mrs. Eulas C. Strong and to my biological mother Mrs. Nadine Carthan. Via them, we reach out to all immediate and extended branches of my adoptive and natural families. With love to my "replacement" Kamau Okembe-RA Kyler Imani and to successor and princess Kandyce Bartee, current studying at the College of the Atlantic in Bar Harbor, Maine. Your father is proud of you. I acknowledge here Ms. Melinda Imani, the mother of them both, without whom obviously they could not have been brought forth or grown so upright.

As a whole, this entire volume is dedicated to my intellectual father, Dr. Israel Tribble R.I. P. of the Florida Endowment Fund and and to the entire McKnight Doctoral Fellowship Family. Dr. Tribble without you there would have been one less revolutionary with a Ph.D. Each of us, the graduates, is your eternal legacy. RIP.

To my friend and brother Dr. David A. Padgett who is the pragmatic voice behind my intellectual vision. A better scholar than I who has allowed me the privilege of sharpening my own cognitive sword at his table

To my friend and brother Ned Felton who has been there as a supporter for my non-academic ventures and has stood by me. Thank you, brother.

Contents

Preface

There is scarcely a single issue more important to human beings than their psychological well-being. And clearly this is even truer for oppressed people, since the most important part of the institutionalization of inferiority is the dialectic between the mental ideology of superiority on the part of the elite and that of inferiority on the part of the masses. Using African people as a tangible example, clearly a defining part of their maafa (meaning "great disaster") as a people and as architects of historical civilization has been the systematic conceptual rendering of their group as "minority," "black," and "slave," among other stigmatizing terms. This is of course, no question of pure semantics, for the terminology is revealing of a deep-seating socio-cultural ideology of antipathy toward African people and their own humanity. One of the perennial side-effects of Platonic materialization and capitalist commodification of social as well as non-social reality has been the need for an epistemological "Other" who stands as the object of socio-psychological projection. The evils and plagues of modernity and society are foisted upon these scapegoats and "whipping boys and girls." Their humanity inextricably "branded" by these scars, they are left unique vampiric and predatory consumers of their own destruction. There is a corollary to the maxim "we have met the enemy and they are we." It goes something like "if the enemy is us (or rendered sociologically as such) then the resurrection of society is based on our own demise. And so "blackness" became the social scientific repository of negativity in the context of white supremacy. Drugs, crime, poverty, all were "blackasized" and then etched into the incarnated Africans among us. This etching is not unique in US history and certainly there are many groups that have borne the burden of discrimination and many varieties. We focus herein on African-Americans simply because their experience is thrown in such stark relief against the traditional US rhetorical template of inclusion.

US psychology, as European colonial psychology before it, was all too eager to serve the elite in codifying "racial" inferiority. The "black" mind was the inferior mind. Standards of normalcy were drawn with reference to upper middle class norms and values. Thus we quickly reached a point in which Guthrie could fairly entitled a masterpiece, Even the Rat Was White, less a reference to the color of the rodents in experimental psychology than a reference to how thoroughly notions of class, caste, and race had rhetoricized psychotherapeutic discourse. As society evolved, many critiqued this perspective from internal and external philosophic angles. Eventually, a synthesis of sorts was reached in the development of ethnic and multicultural psychological approaches.

The ethnic psychologies sought to recognize the unique aspects that the sociological context brings to the psychological moments of members of a group. They were therefore inherently essentialist in their formulation. It had the practical effect of further marginalizing the psychotherapeutic care and theorizing about the mental condition of the oppressed, in desperate need of care. The multicultural psychology sought a wider point of reference, but suffered from the same malady to some degree in that Euro-Americans were perceived as in other social sciences as somehow cultureless and therefore as the "control group." The result was a coalition of the marginalized as opposed to a rethinking of the discipline.

Here, we attempt to critique a multicultural psychotherapeutic moment in a particular common context for the oppressed, and that is in the shadow of judicial directive. We try to point out what the major insights are from a non-Western non-materialist socio-psychological perspective. What is it that these practitioners are missing? Is the program debilitated by the minds of the "clients" or by the minds of the practitioners? What is dysfunctionality? What is normalcy? How much does socio-cultural context matter? Are there any directions we might go in, theoretically and practically, that might make this therapeutic interchange more "successful?"

This work is a not so hidden call for the necessity of a fusion between sociological inquiry and psychological treatment in addressing the critical needs of people, particularly in the context of systems of oppression and coercion. It is also a call for a rigorous examination of non-Western models of psychological functionality as an ameliorative for our current theoretical deficits. I invite you to this ethnographic entrée . . . Bon appetit!

Chapter One

Virtual Reality

The great anti-colonialist psychiatrist Frantz Fanon spoke of the methodologies by which the colonized can internalize the mindset of those who have been their oppressors. This important insight led to a whole critique of psychology and psychotherapeutic methodologies as they were applied to non-Western populations with a theoretical eye towards an explication of how Western psychology has played and continues to play an important role in the mechanisms of Euro-centrism. Among the precedent setting works in this area was the book Even the Rat was White by Guthrie and with respect to African people in particular works like Black Anglo-Saxons by Hare. A response to this set of insights was the introduction of the whole field of "multicultural" psychology which in my opinion, has essentially involved the "integration" of Western psychotherapeutic method by liberal and sometimes not so liberal doses of non-Western concepts and standards. Like oil and water however, the mix often does not take very well in practice, and many have argued in fact for an African-centered psychology for African people. In this book I analyze a case of Eurocentric psychotherapeutic reality, arguing neither for a separatist nor an integrationist psychology, but for a new psychology which is more sociological in its orientation towards the "self" and "normalcy" My proposition is that African critical philosophical insights can be instructive in the endeavor of creating such an approach, although not mutually exclusive in such an ability. What is clear to me and I believe is made clear in the substantive evidence of the situations presented here, is that there must be radical reforms in psychological practice and the conceptualization thereof, if we are engage the discipline across various stratification boundaries. Our failure to do so, I further suggest creates a psychology of oppression that serves neither the "patient" nor the would-be "mental liberator." I refer to these scenarios collectively as "head games" suggesting not a leisure or play, but rather strategic interplays design to construct a specific mental perception of reality in the minds of the subjects of psychotherapy. I am influenced here by the work of critical as well as interpretive sociological theorists who quite eruditely enunciate the manner in which reality can be socially constructed. I am also informed by the Africentric work of Dr. John Henrik Clarke who defined power as "the ability to define a reality and have others respond to it as if it were their own." My suggestion is that the critical problem of Western psychotherapy for the neo-colonized in particular is the fact that certification of one's health tends to be connected with the confirmation by the psychologist of just such responses. To the extent that subjects maintain an alternative worldview, they are likely to be seen as therapeutically resistant and in need of more invasive techniques. In this sense, it is not the subject, but ultimately the researcher-therapist who ultimately lives in the reality constructed by their philosophical assumptions and by those of the Western form of the psychological discipline.

"Virtual" reality is the technology used to create a more substantive interface between humans and computer imagery. It simulates the sensate data that create experience. Ideally, the user employs a set of tools that substitute the simulation for sensory inputs from the natural world. This tool is composed of video images for the eyes, "effectors" for the tactile data, and motion monitors that signal the computer to alter the simulation in sync with body ambulation.

Such a configuration of people and machines raises two critical issues of metaphysics. First, since the simulation can generate experiences that do not exist outside of the simulation, can the computer be said to be creating "reality"? Secondly, if this constructed "reality" can exist outside of the natural world, can it truly be deemed artificial at all? Does it effectively compete with the natural world for moral obligation and the need for scientific inquiry?

Roland Barthes made significant progress towards the answering of this question in Mythologies (1972) in which he intimated that the "natural" reality is itself illusory. What is considered part of natural reality is placed there by political construction and history. Neologisms are born as a consequence of our subconscious acknowledgement that the fixed universe is actually dynamic. Dictionaries are, in this theoretical formulation, partially useless in that they present words as having definitions that are independent of history and politics.

As Benjamin Woolley (1992) points out however, the argument that reality is ambiguous is not necessarily to be perceived as evidence of its lack of existence. It is, in fact, an argument for the simultaneous existence of competing perceptions of reality. When power is considered as part of the equation, the consequences of the hierarchies thereby created between such realities are important as objects of analyses.

ORIGINS OF THE EUROCENTRIC PERSPECTIVE

This bifurcation of knowledge between a dominant paradigmatic approach and one or more competing modes of inquiry has its seed in competing socio-cultural imperatives among human groups. At this point in historical time, Europeans and those of European descent are dominant on the global stage. Their imperatives, socio-cultural objectives, and modes of knowledge inquiry are prioritized over those of unrelated groups and therefore, determine the nature and degree of "deviance" in all spheres of human endeavor.

It is necessary here to note the basic parameters and characteristics of Eurocentric epistemology. Specifically, this means grappling with the intellectual legacy of Plato and his ideas. Platonic influences on Europe's speculative thought have been seminal. Plato laid the foundation for the repudiation of the symbolic sense-the denial of cosmic, intuitive knowledge. Epistemologically, he codified the primacy of the "object," which replaced the "symbol." The universe was no longer to be "experienced."

Reality in this formulation becomes bipolar, beginning with the bifurcated "self." The "thinking, rational self" is said to "know itself" by virtue of its oppositional position relative to its "other," the affective part of the self. Such an "other" is threatening, and consequently an antagonistic, confrontational relationship is constructed between entities. Armstrong (1975) describes it thusly: "We see the world as delicately constructed of both terms in an infinite system of contrasting pairs, and bound together by the tension between them."

The dichotomizing mentality assigns different qualitative evaluations to opposing realities and a stratification of value to all of the realities within a given set or category. This latter process occurs simultaneously with segmentation and compartmentalization of independently derived entities. The possibility of organic, sympathetic, complementary, interdependent or holistic relationships between opposites is eliminated, providing grounds for a collective belief in the legitimacy of the dominance of "superior" forms or phenomena over their respective opposites.

Such a modus operandi in early and later Eurocentric thought leads to analytical, non-synthetic reasoning. The new "self" is identified with "pure thought." The emotionless mind creates proper "objects" of knowledge through the act of controlling that which is phenomenologically inferior.

Everything other than the self is objectified and is subject to control as long as that self is affectively detached. Knowledge becomes a mechanism that facilitates power over the "other."

This mandates the universalization and a reification of "truth" as well as an extreme rationalism that believes everything can be known through this process of objectification and that the resulting data constitute reality. As such, the potential for control is constrained only by the capability of applying objectifying methodology.

This objectifying endeavor becomes the criterion of moral behavior. Intuitive knowledge is devalued because it fails to translate into a method for such control and because its acceptance would validate the ideal of divine (i.e., superhuman) cosmogony and existence of a spiritual realm beyond the control of objective knowledge.

Havelock (1967) presents the process of encoding a language for this worldview as a switch from the Homeric oral mode, relying upon emotional interrelationship between the actor and audience, to Plato's literate, critical mode where abstract descriptive science replaces a concrete language of oral memory. The written symbol becomes authoritative utterance. Reductionist symbols are combined with a non-symbolic linear modality.

Reality is codified in linear, sequential steps. Events are viewed in terms of temporality. Change or movement away from a point in a lineal direction toward another imagined point at positive infinity is "progress." This time line joins past, present, and future where the function of the past and present is to give value to the future by virtue of invidious comparison, and then the future is used as a standard by which the present and the past are evaluated. Any form of cultural behavior is justified in pursuit of this objective. Time is therefore, non-phenomenal and experienced as absolute. This change in the conceptualization of time was a precondition for the ascendancy of Eurocentric science. "Purpose" is taking mankind into the "future."

Nature, in the end, confronts man as alien and is approached with a quantifying mentality viewing the universe as solely material, and infinitely susceptible to control via the operation of a superior minds engaged in positivistic inquiry.

THE PSYCHOLOGICAL APPLICATION OF EURO-CENTRISM

This Eurocentric world view gave rise to an equally reductionist psychology concerned with the categorization, mental measurement, and the establishment of norms. The primary unit of study was the individual, and emphasis was centered on the early years of child development. Differences and diversity from established norms were treated as deviant. Unacceptable thoughts, feelings, and impulses were relegated to the unconscious.

However, revolutionary developments have occurred in Eurocentric psychology such as the existential and human potential movements that emphasize respectively human alienation and the actualization of human consciousness. The net effect of these developments has been to reify the philosophy of individualism. Lasch (1979) points out in his Culture of Narcissism that the freedom engendered by these movements was transformed into a justification for self-indulgence.

TOWARDS A MULTICULTURAL CRITIQUE
OF EUROCENTRIC PSYCHOLOGY

As Barthes' (1972) theoretical perspective would suggest, competing ideas concerning the natural mode of psychological inquiry began to arise as power became more dispersed among social groups. These counter-interpretive approaches arose from groups whose socio-cultural experiences and imperatives deviate from those which defined the core. Among the earliest of these perspectives was the multicultural critique which had its foundation in the post-colonialist discourse going on throughout the sciences. This point of view argued that Eurocentric psychology had been one driving force behind the scientific rationalization of colonialism. As such, it had to be reformulated and recast in an effort to make it inclusive and capable of serving the scientific and medical needs of formerly colonized peoples. This perspective developed from examination of the personality structures of people in crisis. These crises had in common the fact that the subjects felt "different" from those around them. These feelings were accompanied by those of alienation and loneliness and of being misunderstood. The condition is typical among members of socially subordinated groups. The common dynamic in the "different ness syndrome" is mismatch. The victims feel alienated from society. The root lies in cultural and individual differences. The dominant society imposes pressures on individuals to conform, to abandon our individuality, and to force ourselves into the fictional ideal molds and patterns created by those who have power and influence (Katz and Taylor, 1988). This has led to new paradigms as well as to new models of personality and counseling (Comaz-Diaz and Griffith, 1982; Pedersen, 1988).

These new approaches were necessitated, not only by differentiation of the patient constituency, but also by the historical cooptation of the discipline itself by the forces of colonialism and imperialism. France, England, Spain, and Portugal used psychological theory, concepts, and techniques in extensive socio-cultural subversion programs. These programs affected detribalization and enculturation. The objective was to validate the belief that the colonizer's cultures and lives were superior (Collins, 1954) and to replace traditional loyalties with total allegiance to the culture and religion of the colonizer.

American attitudes towards the pursuit of psychological inquiry initially began with a "melting pot" orientation (Crevecoeur, 1904). They became more exclusionary as more people from Eastern Europe, Asia, and Latin America began to immigrate to the United States. This view was articulated by E.P. Cubberly (1909). He stated that the goal of the U.S. educational system was to "break up these groups or settlements, to assimilate and amalgamate these people as part of our American race, and to implant in their children, as far as can be done, the Anglo-Saxon conception of righteousness, law and order and our popular government, and to awaken in them a reverence for our democratic institutions and for those things in our national life which we as a people hold to be of abiding worth." Psychology became subservient to this agenda. One of the tools was the intelligence test as noted by many including Guthrie (1976) in his book, *Even the Rat Was White*. Another was psychoanalytic theory on personality. Freud (1925) concluded that women were not as highly developed as men. Mannoni (1960) concluded that colonization was made possible by an inherent need in subject populations to be dependent. Still another borrowed tool was behavior modification. For example, the misclassification of socially subordinated group members as subject to conduct disorder, oppositional defiant disorder, attention deficit disorder, and learning disabled. A person so characterized is subject to behavior management in schools, prisons, mental hospitals, and in institutions for the mentally ill.

The problems associated with the orthodoxy in psychological diagnosis and treatment lead to the development of opposing views. These came from social forces that had been previously excluded from consideration as generators of psychological theory. One of the first pioneers in the development of this emerging psychology of differentness was Karen Horney. She discovered that the biological orientation of Freud's theory ignored cultural realities involving the powerless position of most women in society and the central role of culture in personality dynamics. George Sanchez (1932) contributed by noting that racial and ethnic superiority based on the results of intelligence tests was illusory, ignoring the environmental and linguistic factors. Frantz Fanon emphasized the importance of socio-cultural realities and the influence of racism and oppression in the personality development of colonized peoples (Bulhan, 1985). He criticized Freud, Jung, and Adler for their Euro-centrism.

Such ideas led to "community psychology" and to the pluralistic approach. Julian Rappaport (1977) presented the paradigm of person and environment fit: respect for human diversity, the right to be different, and the belief that human problems are those of person and environment fit.

Rappaport's theories, in turn, encouraged the conception of a multicultural "person and environment fit" view. It had as its fundamental tenets the idea that:

(1) There are no inferior people, cultures, or groups in terms of gender, ethnicity, race, economics, religion, region, or language,
(2) Problems of maladjustment are the result of a mismatch between people, or between people and their environments,
(3) Every individual, group, or culture has positive contributions to make to personality development and to a healthy adjustment to life,
(4) People who are willing to learn from others and from groups and cultures different from their own, acquire multicultural building blocks which are the bases of multicultural personality development and multicultural identity,
(5) The synthesis and amalgamation of personality building blocks so acquired occurs when the person with multicultural potential works towards the goals of understanding and cooperation among diverse groups and peoples in the context of a pluralistic society, and,
(6) This synthesis results in the development of a multicultural personality and concomitant psychological readjustment.

Associated with this world view is a model of psychotherapy and counseling that emphasizes the idea that:

(1) Every client has the potential for multicultural development,
(2) client origins should be respected as the foundations for multicultural development,
(3) therapists have preferred cultural and cognitive styles,
(4) clients are to be encouraged to take diversity challenges which promote growth and development, and
(5) clients should become active agents in social and personal change.

TOWARDS AN AFRICENTRIC CRITIQUE
OF EUROCENTRIC PSYCHOLOGY

This more open view, fusing Eurocentric psychological principles with post-colonialist models of individual mental fitness and normalcy, was adequate for those having the colonial experience. It seemed inadequate for incorporating the experiential reality of members of the African diaspora in the United States who had endured generations of displacement, enslavement, and segregation. The challenge was not to possession of their land, but to their humanity itself.

An Africentric perspective as the foundation for the psychology of members of the African diaspora in the United States was largely ignored in the first hundred years of formal psychology. When they were mentioned under the general rubric of "negroes," the emphasis was usually on deviance, pathology, and abnormality, using descriptive terms such as impulse-ridden, passive-dependent, disorganized, emotionally immature, poor self-image, self-hatred, identity confusion, psycho-sexual conflicts, and cultural deprivation (Jones 1980).

Wade Nobles (1977) referred to this problem of misdiagnoses in "white" psychology as one involving errors of transubstantiation. Psychologists used a frame of reference developed out of one cultural experience base and attempted without correction to apply this frame of reference to the interpretation of the behavior of people in other cultural frameworks. Psychologists interpreted differences between Africans and Euro-Americans as deviant behavior. (White, 1984)

Traditional Euro-American psychotherapy with African patients, particularly in institutional settings, was coercive in that the therapist imposed his concept of reality on the client in exchange for psychic support and assistance. (Scheff, 1968) Psychotherapists had been trained to view patients as favorable candidates for psychotherapy if they accepted, or could be led to accept, their problems as internal. Patients who accepted that their problems were primarily internal were said to be gaining in insight and received support and favorable progress reports. Patients who insisted that their problems were external were said to be resistant. "Change not the truth." (Yankelovich and Barrett, 1970). Sabshin, et al. (1970), noted that Euro-American psychiatrists were guilty of overemphasizing psychological explanations at the expense of economic and social variables.

Beginning in the 1930s a small number of pioneer African-American psychologists and graduate students began to speak out against this trend in psychology to label Africans as pathological, defective, and mentally inferior. Their efforts are chronicled in Robert Guthrie's *Even the Rat was White* (1976).

The modern era of Africentric psychology officially began in 1968 with the formation of the Association of Black Psychologists. Reginald Jones' Black Psychology (1980) laid out the conceptual requirements of the field of Africentric psychology and the strategies to implement the models. First, the conceptual framework of Africentric psychology designed to organize, explain, and understand behavior should be developed out of the authentic experience base of Africans. It is not possible to explain adequately the behavior of Africans using psychological and conceptual frameworks that have been developed out of the experience base of Europeans (White, 1970). A corollary requirement is that complex mentalist explanations of African behavior should be avoided when a more straightforward observational cause and effect sequence derived from an African experiential-phenomenal discrimination perspective will suffice. Second, the psychology of "Blackness" should concentrate on the strengths Africans have used to survive, revitalize, and actualize, and "keep on keepin' on" under the oppressive conditions of life. Third, the search for truth should not be limited to narrow, statistical criteria only. Consensual validation, oral history, intuitiveness, and the word of the people as witnesses of their own direct experience should all be considered as legitimate evidence.

TOWARDS AN AFRICAN GLOBAL CRITIQUE OF EUROCENTRIC PSYCHOLOGY

As African consciousness in the United States expanded in such a manner that it perceived the diasporic experience of Africans in the United States as part of the total collective historical experience of African people overall, modes of psychological inquiry had to be developed which perceived the central locus of well-being and mental health as existing at the level of that collective. The African-centered critique is the result.

African theoreticians questioned the application of traditional Eurocentric treatment approaches to African populations, citing as evidence the lack of congruence of these practices with African experience, life style, and culture (Akbar, 1977; W. Allen, 1978; Amini, 1972; Buck, 1977; Leonard and Jones, 1980; G. Jackson, 1976). Models of personality and treatment based on African frames of reference have been proposed as corrective mechanisms by certain theoreticians (Jones, 1980; Toldson and Pasteur, 1975).

Psychological theories provide a mechanism for understanding human behavior and for developing treatment models. However, these theoretical formulations are germane only to the extent that the importance of culture is recognized and relevant cultural values incorporated (Hall, 1977). Cultural theories in African psychology are characterized generally by an emphasis on "wellness" or normality instead of psychopathology. Notably absent are concepts of disordered development and a reliance on individual recompensation, except as individual efforts are influenced by group goals or extended self-identity (Baldwin, 1976; A. Jackson 1982; Mbiti, 1971; Nobles 1976).

The salient value of African culture and lifestyle in treatment approaches have been addressed increasingly by African psychologists (A. Jackson, 1982; Jones, 1980; Toldson and Pasteur, 1975). The incorporation of cultural values in treatment is advocated by many practitioners (Akbar, 1977; A. Jackson, 1982).

The Africa-centered psychological model involves the consideration of four variables: (a) the degree of impact white colonialism and supremacy has upon the lives of Africans, (b) the degree to which a particular African psychological perspective is a marker of strength rather than weakness, (c) language styles, and (d) the affect cultural differences have on the nature of appropriate therapeutic strategies.

Psychiatrist Alfred Memmi (1965) states that psychological freedom of the oppressed can only come from their definition as independent of the "master." Dr. Francis Cress Welsing, another psychiatrist, identifies white world supremacy as "the local and global power system structured and maintained by persons who classify themselves as 'white,' whether consciously or subconsciously determined." She goes on to describe the system as consisting of "patterns of perception, logic, symbol formation, thought, speech, action and emotional response, as conducted simultaneously in all areas of people activity" (Welsing 1991). The rage, distrust, and sorrow engendered by more than four centuries of victimization in the United States is legitimate, likely to be expressed in the therapeutic situation, and cannot simply be explained away as evidence of severe maladjustment or neurotic manifestations of transference (Grier and Cobbs, 1968). Therapists have to avoid the "great white father" syndrome in which they take an omnipotent position knowing what's best for the client, that their judgment is superior, and believing that their client should passively submit to their advisements [with gratefulness for their benevolence] (Vontress, 1971).

There are six recurring psychological themes in the expressive patterns of Africans:

(1) emotional vitality
(2) "realness"
(3) resilience
(4) interrelatedness
(5) the value of direct experience, and
(6) distrust and deception.

There is a sense of aliveness, animation, emotional vitality and openness to feelings expressed in the oral and body languages of Africans (Redmond, 1971). African oral language is described by Jeffers (1971) as being vivacious, exuberant, sensuous, and wholesomely uninhibited. In the African oral tradition, the act of speaking is a performance on the stage of life (Holt 1975). To capture and hold the attention of the listener, the speaker is expected to make the words come alive, to use ear-filling phrases that stir the imagination with heavy reliance on tonal rhymes, symbolism, figures of speech, and personification. The vitality expressed in the language is life-affirming: despair, apathy, and downtrodden ness are rejected.

The first step of learning to survive in the African experience is to see life exactly as it is, without self-deception or romantic pieties (Neal 1972). In the African ethos tragedy, defeat and disappointment are not equated with psychological destruction. Psychological growth and emotional maturity cannot be completed until the person has paid his or her dues by overcoming hardship, defeat, sorrow, and grief (Baldwin, 1963).

The consciousness of pain, sorrow, and hurt among Africans can be differentiated from the clinical syndrome of depression where guilt, shame, and anger are transformed into self-depreciation work against the serenity of sadness. The openness to a balanced spectrum of emotions in African consciousness makes it easier to draw upon the revitalization powers of sensuousness, joy, and laughter.

In the theoretical model of Africa-centered psychology presented by Wade Nobles (1976) interrelatedness, connectedness, and interdependence are viewed as the unifying philosophic concepts. It is important to note here that the structure of psychology is similar to that of medicine in that many practitioners are simultaneously academics and entrepreneurs. That is, all of the academics referenced here are also therapists and practicing psychologists. Their practices are either private or affiliated with their respective academic institutions.

These are prominent themes in African language with respect to the interactive dynamics between speaker and listener, the power of words to control, cognitive style, timing, and communicative competence. The spoken word is the pervasive force that connects human experiences. These linkages are established across time and space. The act of speaking is a dramatic presentation of one's personhood to those who share a background of similar acculturation (Holt, 1975). The call and response dialogue style, where the listener acts as an echo chamber, repeating, cosigning, validating, and affirming the message of the speaker, joins two or more individuals in a common psycholinguistic space. Each participant expands the message through amplification and repetition. The interactive balance between the linguistic rhythms of the speaker and listener is synchronized by a reciprocal command of timing and pace. The goal is to be in time with the beat, pulse, tempo, and rhythm of the speech flow. The African speaker establishes a form of situational control vis-à-vis the listener by defining a reality using vivid imagery drawn from a body of collective experiences that others understand and can relate to events in their life space (Holt, 1975). Speakers depend on the common background between themselves and the listeners to establish impact and associate meanings to the words. The intellectual meaning is carried by implication creating a psycho-affective or cognitive and affective synthesis (Smitherman, 1977). The speaker controls the situation linguistically with words that touch rhythms stemming from such syntheses, activating emotions and feelings. The extensive use of metaphor in African speech reflects a cognitive style where likeness, correspondence, similarity, and analogous relationships between ideas, events, and concepts are shown by using picturesque imagery that appeals both to the intellect and emotions. Signifying symbols in the form of visual imagery are substituted for abstract concepts to explain and clarify meanings. This imagery stimulates the power of the mind to see, to visualize abstract relationships, and to project novel interpretations (Holt, 1975). Metaphorical expressions generate multiple meanings. The cultural connotation is conveyed by translating the expression or figure of speech through an ethno tropic filter delineated by an Africa-centered world view. The specific meaning of a statement in a given situation is dependent on contextual clues, coupled with cultural sophistication and innovativeness of the participants. [Ethno tropism is the use of a word, phrase, or utterance in a different cultural context for the purpose of giving life or emphasis to an idea] (Holt, 1975).

There is no substitute in the African ethos for actual experiences gained in the course of living. A person lacking in mother wit, the common sense of experiences, who flaunts untested book knowledge is perceived in the African-American idiom as an educated fool. Another central theme is a result of the negative experience of Africans at the hands of Europeans. This involves a sense of distrust and a communicative style for deceiving "the man." The use of a common language with culturally different semantics enables Africans to conceal what they mean from Europeans while still maintaining a high level of clarity in their communications. Words, phrases, and statements that are taken to mean one thing when interpreted from a Eurocentric frame of reference can mean something entirely different when translated through an Africa-centered ethno tropic filter. Linguistic deception can be used as a way of controlling undesirable psychological imagery and evaluative labels propagated by Europeans.

The maintenance of support systems and interdependent relationships with others is a sign of ego strength in African patients (Block, 1980). Therapists who work with them should provide their clients with knowledge of community support groups that can assist with legal aid, child care, financial benefits, employment, and other social services.

The Africa-centered clinical practice model is one of collective action of African professionals, of continuity of services, and of direct intervention within multiple systems. The concept is one of a service chain that encompasses the African client, family members, the African community, and political and economic systems in which the person is involved. The client's worldview, cultural environment, and situational context would be integral parts of the assessment procedure. The emphasis is on holistic health and prevention rather than disease. Problems are assumed to have multiple origins and to require multiple approaches for solution. The model is composed of seven basic modules- The African helping person, the African client and family, African professionals, the African community, African culture, political and economic systems, and the general environment. All modules are essential, but the primary units are the first two. The initial role of the helping professional is one of understanding the problems that have developed in the system, helping the client understand the difficulty, and ultimately, to facilitate behaviors that will lead to better functioning involving multiple relationships within the system. Change of any kind must involve factors that influence behavior and the quality of life. Another important facet of the model is the close working relationships among African professionals. Optimal mental health involves synchrony between Africaneity in identity, in culture, and in genealogy.

OBJECTIVES AND METHODS OF THIS RESEARCH PROJECT

This is an ethnographic evaluation study of a psychotherapy program, targeted at first time law violators and their families. The program had failed to accomplish its goals which were to address presumed dysfunctionalities in familial structure deemed generative of illegality. My research study focused on analysis of the theory, methodology, and practice of the program with respect to its consideration for the socio-cultural context of African-Americans. The African-American socio-cultural context was selected because all of the families and offenders in the program are African-American. The hypothesis was that the program failed to consider the socio-cultural experience of African-Americans and that this omission served a purpose in programmatic expansion and replication.

In developing a methodological approach for examining the aforementioned hypothesis, I found the "virtual reality" metaphor powerful. First, the fundamental metaphysical questions raised by the technology surface in this analysis as epistemological and ontological queries. Are the psychotherapy practitioners creating a paradigmatic reality for themselves, as a consequence of their insensitivity to the dictates of a different socio-culture and their commitment to a Eurocentric psychotherapeutic approach? Do the participants or "patients" exist in a different and competing experiential reality than the one suggested by the staff's paradigm?

Second, the sensory substitution necessary for making the simulation work in the minds of the virtual reality user are analogous to similar replacements made by the Eurocentric psychological epistemology and ontology, as implemented by the staff, in order to perpetuate the evaluations and/or definitions of dysfunctionality. The latter are used as tools of legitimation and self-rationalization for one's participation in the therapeutic effort. Since they are foundational, competing observations and perspectives must be nullified or subsumed within them. Just as a simulation which fails to effectively insulate the user from external, competing sensory impressions will fail to motivate him or her from acceptance of the computer world as real, failure of a theoretical paradigm to negate competing knowledge bases will raise fundamental questions about the reality of its assertions and the validity of information it purports to provide.

Since my inquiry was one focused on competing perceptions of reality and inter-subjectivity, I decided upon investigative field research and ethnographic participant observation as my primary mode of data collection. These were triangulated with interview data gathered periodically from program staff and quantitative data that were being collected by the staff in order to solicit further grant funding for the program.

Investigative field research has its emphasis on direct personal observation, interaction, and experience (Douglas 1976). My goal was to understand the programmatic world from the perspective of the participants and the organizers (Blumer 1969). Ethnography was selected as the mode of choice primarily because of its flexibility. The grounded theory methodology facilitates a constant dialogue between data, data collection, and data analysis. It facilitates the changing of strategy and direction of research in the face of changing developments at the site level in line with what may be required by theory construction. Ideas can be "tested" as it were, and if beneficial, pursued. Moreover, ethnography allows theory development to be pursued with a high degree of effectiveness and economy.

Ethnography also contains the ability to test theory. Cases that are crucial may be examined. There is a reduced risk of ecological invalidity. The method is inherently triangulated with multiple data sources weaved into the accounts avoiding another difficulty, methodological dependency. Examples of the application of ethnography in this regard are provided by Hargreaves (1967), Lacey (1970), and Ball (1981).

The participant observation data in this study were self-compiled and were drawn from my attendance at hour-long youth therapy sessions as well as from combined parent and youth sessions which immediately followed and lasted an hour. Complementing these data were systematic notes gathered during my attendance at the weekly program staff meetings at which critical assessments were made of the preceding week's therapy program.

Access

As the work of Barbera-Stein (1979) illustrates, a critical issue in ethnographic research is the process of access negotiation. She describes it "as involving multiple views of what is profane and open to investigation vs. what is sacred or taboo and closed to investigation unless the appropriate respectful stance or distance is assumed." Informal sponsorship becomes an essential element and may be gained through the mobilization of existing social networks based on acquaintanceship, kinship, or occupational membership. In formal organizations, initial access negotiations may be focused on formal permission that can be legitimately granted or withheld by key personnel. These individuals are often the initial point of contact within the setting for the ethnographer. Such gatekeepers will generally be concerned as to the picture of the organization the ethnographer will compose and have interests in this portrayal being favorable and safeguarding their legitimate concerns. They may accordingly exercise some surveillance and control prerogative by fractionating access or steering fieldwork. The ethnographer often falls prey to being represented as an "expert," who is extremely well versed in "problems" and "solutions." He or she thus becomes a "critic" or evaluator. This may lead to support, but may hamper activity since unfavorable impressions or preliminary reports of the same may interfere with the subsequently granted access.

All of these points are relevant in my own project. As a result of my initial inquiries concerning conducting research on the program, I had been referred to Dr. Wind, the faculty member supervising the activities of the mental health clinic and one of the principal investigators for the program I was interested in. This initial contact took the form of a meeting in Dr. Wind's office. Dr. Wind went through a summary of the program and distributed textual material on its official theoretical and epistemological foundations and structure. He also introduced me to the graduate students who had the role of counselors in the program and who ran the individual and collective sessions with the parents and the youth. He gave us a rigorous guided tour of the facilities in the office of the department and in the clinic next door. Moreover, he expressed his willingness to facilitate any meetings and procurement of data that would make me successful in my endeavor. One important point is that at the end of the presentation, Dr. Wind stated that he hoped my respective research project would provide some useful information for the program. As for the finer details of access, for example, the type of information that could be gathered and by what appropriate methods, I was referred to Dee, the student program director. The federal grant program which financed my research authorized the use of our collected data for academic papers, conferences, theses, dissertations, and the like.

I first attended the first weekly staff meeting which focused on the arrival of a group of three undergraduate students who, by virtue of signing up to do independent work in the areas of clinical psychology and social work, were to have some role in the conduct and development of the program. This gave me an opportunity to meet them, them an opportunity to meet me, and an opportunity for us to exchange information about our respective motivations for being in the site. This staff meeting came to take on a greater significance each week as it was a major forum for concerns of the staff about inadequacies of the program and for evaluating the success or failure of the preceding week's activities. It also gave me an opportunity to gain insight into the processes by which individuals were "trained" to work in the program. The undergraduates were temporary functionaries in the program who assumed important roles in its continuance. Because of discussions that arose out of this meeting, it was agreed that I should attend either the youth or the parental session during the time the two groups were separated, but not both. This was out of fear that my movement back and forth might destabilize the therapy sessions. I did not consider this a major sacrifice, although I would have liked to have made some comparative analysis of the separate sessions. I raised other issues like whether or not there was an existing base of qualitative data that I might use as triangulating elements [there were not] and whether any audio or video recording could be made of the proceedings [there could not be, due to the confidentiality and some apprehension on the part of the counselors concerning raising the issue with the participants].

I met Dee, the graduate student who headed the program, at five p.m. on the evening of my first session to ask about the more scientific parameters of the work. She gave me an introduction to the program as she saw it and offered to facilitate any additional qualitative research gathering that I wished to undertake. When I mentioned the concerns that were raised earlier in the meeting, she suggested that my participation would not involve as much interference in the therapy sessions as had been suggested. She offered to allow me to introduce myself to the collective group of participants and to serve as the conduit for my legitimate entry. I made it clear that I wanted to leave any expanded research agenda decisions until after the first observation and that I thought it necessary that I make as little note of my role as a researcher as possible in order not to intimidate either counselors or participants. She did in fact; allow me to introduce myself to the counselors and participants during the evening session.

The next facilitator in the process of my successful entry into the site was Geraldine, an African-American woman and one of two counselors scheduled for duty on that evening. She made a point of including me in the discussions of the group as little as possible [usually when there was an extended lull on the part of the regular participants], facilitating my compilation of detailed notes.

Field Relations

Impression Management

Personal appearance can be a very salient factor in managing impressions of the researcher at the site. In addition, demeanor becomes the instrument by which the delicate balance is struck between the necessary reduction of social differences between the researcher and the subject(s) and the need to maintain some "objective" scholarly distance from him/her (them). There may be different categories of participants and different contexts which necessitate one's becoming a "stylistic chameleon" sensitive to need to vary one's impression management strategy. The construction of such a working identity or of a series of them can be facilitated by researcher exploitation of his or her prior skills. These may include superior technical knowledge and resources. Important also are conformity to the requirements of tact, courtesy, and "interaction ritual" (Goffman, 1972).

Next in the realm of impression management issues are those targeted at avoiding as much as possible biases in the selection of data sources in the field. A researcher cannot confine his or her communication solely to those people whose behavior is agreeable or who are deemed friends (Hammersley 1983c).

Field Roles

One of the most critical errors a field worker can make is to begin treating an established research role as rigid and fixed in character (Turner 1962). Frequently, shifts in role can be made over the course of fieldwork. Indeed, there are strong arguments for just such a strategic manipulation to avoid role-dependent data. Excess rapport with one group may lead to problems in maintaining or developing rapport with others (Miller 1952). The ethnographer must be intellectually poised between familiarity and strangeness, while socially he or she must be poised between stranger and friend (Powermaker 1966; Everhart 1977). All of these considerations informed my own ethnographic inquiry.

My Experience in Field Roles

I decided early on that it would be best for my role to remain as discreet as possible. I avoided directly approaching individuals and admitting that I was studying them, but instead took the role of the "Socratic" questioner, who was naive and always needed additional information about things. There was that matter of initial self-introduction as an observer and a doctoral student, but in a very short time it appears that familiarity with me, developed by my presence within the sessions, led to a removal of any discomfort this knowledge may have given program staff members or participants. At least no concern over this matter was mentioned to me or to any of the program officials. My role was rather an anomaly in the sense that I was a peer to neither the professionals nor the program participants. The patients seemed to see my role as a potential sounding board for their concerns. On the other hand, to the supervisors of the project, I was a potential future source of information that could provide a useful critique and evaluation of the goings-on. My role with them was along the lines of Goffman's (1963) wise individual who gains a tolerated courtesy membership, running the risk of the stigma associated with such a position, and being often forced to conceal the nature and/or results of the research from the individuals involved in the social interaction being studied.

In my overt posture, I showed interest in the research of the principal investigators and in the work of the counselors, encouraging them to talk about their perspectives. My access to the patients, for reasons previously discussed, was somewhat more limited but via empathetic body language in the collective sessions and sympathetic words in the youth sessions, I sought to encourage them to elucidate their positions and feel secure in the knowledge of revealing them in my presence. I worked to develop their trust.

My process of gaining trust, like that of gaining entry, was facilitated by the enthusiasm with which the principal investigators of the project and key counselors greeted my arrival. They acted as gatekeepers, easing my path towards gaining the trust of all concerned. As I continued the research project however, I began to be concerned that this initial trust constituted a risk, as some of my findings were not consistent with the perception that the sponsors had of their own program. A "web of trust" (Douglas 1976) is not a one-time phenomenon, but an ongoing developmental process (Johnson 1975). Nor is it a one-way process, but can be diminished, withdrawn, rearticulated, and re-questioned at any point (Carey 1972; Douglas 1972). I wondered what the effect would be on my access to the site and relevant officials in the event of their knowledge of my developing critique. Consequently, I took care to steer clear of direct questions concerning my impressions, directing them instead back upon the questioners so that they might provide additional relevant information and fill in gaps within my emerging conceptual landscape.

A methodological issue arose from the cultural clash between me and the psychology graduate students that constituted a major part of my subject constituency. Other sociologists have also noted these differences (Humphreys 1970; Whyte 1955). As a researcher seeks to get in-depth information from subjects, he or she is likely to come across fundamental differences in character, values, and attitudes between their subjects and themselves. In my case, I was confronted by differences in the degree of epistemological acceptance of the socially constructed notion of deviance as an analytical and prescriptive tool, particularly involving African-Americans. This ontological gap caused me at times anger and exasperation. I watched the clinicians "act out" a program that was not only often degrading to the participants, but that was likely to have little or no impact on the stated goals of reducing the potential for criminality or antisocial behavior among the youth. I resisted the frequent desire to leave my more detached, primarily observational role and to defend my African-American brothers and sisters from what I at times perceived to be a psychosocial engineering project.

This lack of involvement, likewise, gave rise to a personal ethical dilemma as to whether or not I was obligated to intervene in cases where the therapy reached a point of degradation of the participants. Like other researchers, I felt the pangs of guilt associated with not acting on my personal will (Carey 1972; Douglas 1976; Humphreys 1970; Johnson 1975; Klockars 1977, 1979; Rochford 1985). This became especially important during the writing up of this research as I became concerned about whether to reveal the identities of the psychological staff, who could suffer professionally and otherwise from the findings. I was torn by the knowledge that it was necessary that these findings be known for the benefit of all African-Americans who generally constitute the target constituency for such programs, as well as those who facilitate the continuation of such projects in terms of research, publication, staffing, and funding under the false hope that they address the underlying "deviance" problems that are the foci of their concern.

Insider Accounts

Participant observation knowledge on the part of the subjects being examined by an ethnographer can be an asset. Despite one's skill at being able to negotiate a role that facilitates perception of events, one may be denied some component of information not available firsthand. Individuals may be cultivated (Bigus 1972) or "trained" (Paul 1953) as informants.

All human behavior has an expressive dimension. Ecological arrangements, clothes, gesture, and manners all convey messages about people. In addition, there is the expressive power of language with its capacity to present description, explanation, and evaluation of phenomena. Often language is used in communications by participants under scientific observation to "tell the researcher how it is" (Hammersley 1980; Hitchcock 1983). The influence of cognitive assumptions leads many ethnographers to discount such perspectives as "less valid" (Becker and Geer, 1960). Others argue that rather than approaching the issue from the validity perspective one should focus instead on the data as data that inform the researcher about the contextualized perception of reality on the part of the participant offering the information and gives rise to inferences about the context itself (Dean and Whyte 1958).

The stakes involved in the program made me feel extremely cautious about the validity of any material that I gathered from the "professionals." For the graduate student counselors, the program, their involvement, and their success within that context involved vital issues like grades, hour credit, practicum completion for doctorates, admission to graduate programs, and research funding. To address this potential bias, I employed a bifurcated method. First, I tested interview data compiled from various program staff members and from the principal investigators against the textual imperatives of the program as recorded in its supporting documentation. I adopted an attitude consistent with a suspicion of the existence of vested interests whenever there was a discrepancy between textually stated objectives and verbally stated objectives of the individuals involved, between textual description and subjective reality as defined by the staff members themselves. Secondly, my observations of the scene constituted a primary resource. I was involved with many of the principals on a weekly basis and was attending all therapy sessions and review meetings. I could contrast what was being said with what I could see was taking place. Frequently, I noted counselors' and administrators' evasions and misperceptions through incongruities between words and their actions. Throughout the research, I used these crosschecking measures to evaluate the veracity of new information.

In ethnography, theory construction and data gathering are dialectically linked, the latter being guided strategically by the former (Glaser and Strauss 1967). This involves a comparative method in which each segment of data is taken in turn, its relevance to one or more theoretical categories noted, and its comparison with other data segments similarly categorized. The range and variation of any category can be mapped accordingly in the data.

The Setting

Before turning to the analysis itself, it is necessary to develop a demographic and structural profile of the program. This includes examination of the program objectives, its theoretical orientation, and its target constituency.

The first offenders program is funded by the [Southern state] Youth and Coordinating Council. The principal investigators for the project are Dr. Quaser and Dr. Wind, faculty at [Southern state university]. It is described in its mission statement as "a diversion program that provides an alternative disposition for children at the time of their first arrest for misdemeanor conduct." It identifies its target population as children and parents who are referred to the program by the Juvenile Probation Department which acts upon the child's arrest and/or receipt of misdemeanor citations. The families, I was informed by program staffers, had come to the program by consent and were presumed to have pledged beforehand to complete the program in a satisfactory manner. The program consists of a two hour and thirty minute meeting once a week for a period of eight weeks. The format involves a small group discussion led by facilitators, followed by a group presentation on the same or similar topics.

Theoretical Orientation of the Program

The facilitators in the program are charged with the responsibility of practicing skill-building techniques, promoting discussion of the issues by youth and parents, providing clarity of concepts presented in the large group, and giving a focus for youth and parents to problem solve personal family issues. The program tries to create a context that encourages family members to develop and implement solutions for their own families. The program views the family as the agent of change and seeks to strengthen family bonds and interrupt dysfunctional patterns, largely as a consequence of the psychological theory orientation of the principal investigators. It is predicated upon the belief that intervention with children and parents on the first contact with the Juvenile Justice System provides a greater opportunity for change than would otherwise be yielded from latter efforts.

Theoretically, its foundations include the work of de Shazer (1985, 1988), Selenkman (1991), and O'Hanlon and Weiner-Davis (1989), all of whom explored some aspect of solution oriented parenting group therapy as an alternative to traditional treatment methodologies. Solution focused therapy rests on the foundation that the clients themselves possess the resources for solving life's problems. The focus of this school of therapy is to bring into the foreground the times that the problem is not present and highlight times when the client is successful in his or her activities.

The program makes use of the body of psychological theory that suggests families are better capable of grappling with problems when their ideas are voiced collaboratively [Andersen (1988), Anderson and Goolishan (1988), and White and Epston (1990)]. This allows, theoretically at least, for a high degree of flexibility in the program in terms of feedback and adaptability given the availability of the perspectives of several families on issues. The emphasis could therefore be upon issues deemed important for the relevant community and the therapeutic encounter could be wholly experiential.

White and Epston (1990) were particularly instructive for their strategy of psychotherapeutic externalization. Externalizing is a theoretical approach to psychotherapy that encourages persons to objectify and personify the problems they experience as oppressive. The problem thereby becomes a separate entity rendering inherent problems less fixed and restrictive. As a result, the individual (s) concerned can eliminate the problem as an essential part of their subjective descriptive narratives of lived experience. The latter are constitutive of lives in the sense that they ascribe experiential meaning and select aspects of life for emphasis and mental re-visitation. The assumption of this paradigm is that by the process of controlling for this newly externalized problematic factor, positive and unique sub-narratives of individual lived experience are made visible, given voice, and can provide bases for potential new articulation of life experience and new modes of self-improvement.

This externalization is affected by relative influence questioning of the individual involving two interrogative components. The first encourages individuals to describe the influence of the problem on their lives. The second encourages them to describe their own influence on the problem during its lifespan.

Demographic Profile of the Program

One hundred and ninety-one "first offenders" were assessed. First offenders were defined by the program as individuals who were first-time lawbreakers. The age of the youth ranged from six to sixteen years with a mean of thirteen. Eighty-six percent of the group was African, thirteen percent Euro-American, and one percent Hispanic/Latino. Sixty-seven and one-half percent of the subjects were male. Fifty-two percent came from single parent households, twenty-six percent from two parent households, and twenty-one percent from two adult (one parent) households. The median school grade for the sample was precisely between the seventh and eighth grades.

Regarding age at first referral to juvenile justice, twenty-nine percent were twelve years of age or younger, nineteen percent were thirteen years of age, and fifty-two percent were between fourteen and sixteen.

School functioning was assessed in the risk assessment by gathering data on retention, detention, suspensions, grades, courses failed or then failing, and attendance. Thirty-five percent of the sample showed evidence of recent grade or behavior problems in school. Chronic school problems, several years in duration, along with behavior problems, were found to occur in forty-nine percent of the cases. Two percent of the cases were drop outs. Thirteen percent of the cases involved no school problems.

For eighty-two of the youth, data on grades, number of suspensions, and number of unexcused absences had been collected. The average number of subjects failing for this group was three, number of unexcused absences is ten or more, and average number of suspensions is four. Seventeen youth were failing in all of their subjects, while twelve were failing in none of their subjects.

An assessment was conducted on youth alcohol and drug use. In sixty-eight percent of the cases, no drug or alcohol use was found. In twenty-five percent of the cases, experimental and/or occasional use was found. In seven percent of the cases, substantial use and possible dependence was found.

Finally, criminal involvement in the family was assessed. Criminal involvement was the conviction of one or more family members of a criminal offense. The level of seriousness was determined by the number of family members involved and the number of incidents involved. In seventy-one percent of the cases, no involvement or minor criminal involvement was found. In twenty-five percent of the cases, a moderate level of criminal involvement in the family had occurred sometime in its history. In four percent of the cases, serious criminal involvement had occurred.

Overview

In the following chapters, I examine the internal logic of the program as I saw it, experienced it, and learned of it through conversations with others involved at various positions within the structure of the endeavor. The program was organized, yet intricate, and influenced by a variety of diverse and often conflicting factors.

Here I have introduced the people, setting, and basic types of activities inherent in this social world. In chapters 2 through 6, I present an analysis of what occurred in the program during the period of my observation, [involving the independent youth counseling sessions, the joint youth and parent sessions, and the weekly program meeting], outlining the basic modus operandi for the program from the point of view of the offenders, their families, the program's principal investigators, counselors, and undergraduate assistants through their behavior in and out of the sessions, their instructional training and texts, and their informal interviews with me. I address the processes by which they respectively come into the program, how that influences the manner in which they perceive themselves, the program and other participants and the behavior that they each manifest.

In chapter seven, my conclusion, I endeavor to theoretically explain the manner in which the program fails to liberate African families from their presumed psychological problems in the manner suggested by its documentary material and by the statements of program staff and the principal investigators.

Chapter Two

"Mind-Space"

In his 1986 novel, *Neuromancer*, William Gibson introduced the term "cyberspace." He described it as a "consensual hallucination," a point at which the consciousness of an individual merges entirely with media. I use the derivative term "mind-space" in the context of my research to characterize the "consensual hallucination" of the therapeutic moment I evaluated and as inculcated in the thoughts, actions, and statements of the therapists. Their consciousness merged with a dominant narrative discourse in psychotherapy which identifies the "patients" (rendered as subjects) as "dysfunctional." This orientation also involved a positivistic view of the potential for psychotherapeutic treatment of the participants.

The program operated with little apparent recognition of the essential validity of the participants' worldviews and definitions of the "reality," all the while failing to be self-reflective with respect to its own epistemological and ontological grounding in a mono-cultural perspective. The operational dictum seemed to be rooted in a longstanding tradition in Euro-centric psychological theory and that is the presumption that the same basic processes underlie all human thought. Cultural differences in such a formulation might dictate the subject of thought, but the habits of thought were presumed to be the same. Among these habits would have been traditionally included a devotion to logical reasoning, a penchant for categorization, and a linear understanding of causality. But as Dr. Richard Nisbett at the University of Michigan and other researchers have found, people who grow up in different cultural contexts not only think about different things, but they think differently. Western thought, in particular is characterized by a malady commonly known as the fundamental attribution error in which human behavior is explained in terms of traits of individual actors, even when there is an overriding situational context at work. Within Western psychological theory this leads to an important breach between social psychology and individual psychology that can and does, as this project will demonstrate lead to misdiagnoses (Goode, 2000).

From an Africentric standpoint, the therapist must be recognized as a person who has been socialized in a particular cultural framework with a specific values system, and therefore not as an "objective, detached observer" (Schiele, 1996). Recognizing the social position of the therapist and whether or not the "client" shares that framework and systems of values is within the context of an Africentric multicultural psychotherapeutic approach, the problematic rather than an artifact of the therapeutic context.

THE LAY OF THE CONCEPTUAL LAND

The first event I attended as a part of my work at the field site involved meeting Dr. "Wind." He began by giving me an introduction to the program. Right at the very beginning, he clued me in to the potential for there to be a degree of inconsistency in the program. He stated that the program was formally designed for first offenders between the ages of thirteen and fifteen, but pointed out that due to errors in referral youth out of that age range were admitted. Moreover, the definition of "first offender" proved to be a very slippery concept. It included a large number of truants as well as some with multiple prior offenses. Dr. Wind stated explicitly that the goal of the program was to promote "positive, healthy, family interactions." He emphasized the fact that the strictly psycho-educational component was a small part of the project with the greater emphasis on familial interaction and sharing. As an incentive, youth who completed the program had their records cleared. The rate of recidivism however, was given as fifty percent, a rather high figure for a program whose mentor was billing it as "successful." He listed as evidence for this "success" a qualitative analysis study, commissioned by the staff research team, which conducted four in-depth case studies of families that had completed the program, finding that for the families studied there were more positive familial relationships and better behavior on the part of the youth.

Admission to the program was predicated upon a forty-five minute risk assessment interview which evaluated the youth in terms of peer group, school records, familial criminal history, and the adequacy of peer groups. I asked for a copy of the risk assessment form [as I thought it crucial to understanding the process of familial entry], and received a promise from Dr. Wind that one would be forthcoming. This proved to be more difficult to get than it first appeared [only one person involved with the program appeared to have a copy and no one could ever seem to produce one for my benefit]. Dr. Wind also stated that the program assigned the first offender families into related support programs as needed. Among these were a youth educational tutorial program and a family therapy program for those considered to need more thorough counseling. Dr. Wind also alluded to the difficulties involved in getting parents and/or guardians of the youth to participate. He then went on to introduce the staff. He suggested that for further definition of the specifics of my research position within the sessions, I should consult "Dee," the head counselor, and that I should attend the weekly meeting for counselors and aides that would next occur on the following day.

THE NARRATIVE DOCUMENTATION OF THE PROGRAM

In the course of the meeting, Dr. Wind provided an enormous amount of research material related to the program and two of the in-depth interviews that were part of the case studies mentioned earlier. I set myself to the task of studying the material and putting it into theoretical perspective. I had in mind two research questions: (1) Why does a program that is presented as being relatively successful have such a poor record in terms of recidivism and parental cooperation, and (2) Why does there appear to be so little access to the materials on risk assessment which, given Dr. Wind's description of the program, constitutes such a major determinant of the therapeutic approach?

The first document I reviewed was a handout on the family program composed as part of a paper delivered at a conference by Dr Wind and Dr. "Quaser" (a second principal-investigator). On the first page there was a flow chart which described the official manner in which families came to be in the program. It began with a judicial review process, where complaints were reviewed at intake. Based upon this initial evaluation, cases were selectively referred to the first offender assessment program. Next, a quantitative risk assessment and risk profile are developed, leading to referral along an increasing continuum of intervention areas. These ranged from no intervention for the low scorers to simultaneous intervention in the areas of familial communication, life skills, school, and nurturing skills for high scorers. The culmination of the program involved a probationary period and then "dispositional referral to programs." The range of scores allowed for considerable therapeutic discretion in the assignment of treatment(s).

On the next page of this conference paper I found the first formal reference to the first offender program. The paper had been introduced as pertaining to the "family" program. It became clear to me over time that two programs had actually been merged into one. The document asserted that the families had "consented to attend and complete the program in a satisfactory manner" and warned that "Those families and/or children who do not attend or become disruptive will be referred back to the probation office for appropriate follow-up." Why would parents and/or guardians who had made such a commitment then renege and refuse to participate or become "disruptive"? The program sought to "interrupt dysfunctional patterns," presumably in the behavior of the children or in the familial structure. Clearly, this indicated a presumption of preexisting "dysfunctionality" as defined by some criteria. The last line stated that the program would "develop a context that encourages family members to develop and implement solutions for their own families." What was curious to me about this was the fact that the families concerned had just been labeled as "dysfunctional."

The last section of the paper was a weekly breakdown of the program and the handouts associated with each week's activities. I noticed a systematic contrast in the paper between the structured, deterministic approach imposed upon the subjects, on the one hand, and the open, fluid approach emerging from their interests and concerns on the other.

The second publication I received from Dr. Wind was a more condensed three page version of the program description, focusing more on its theoretical foundations.

The third and fourth sets of material were interviews conducted with families that had completed the program. Several excerpts from these two interview transcriptions helped to elaborate upon or establish lines of inquiry that I would pursue in subsequent discussions with the staff and in my observations. In each case, the respondent was the parent of an individual who had been judicially referred to the program by the administering judge as a first offender as an alternative to further punitive sanction. Among them:

Parent: They weren't interested in what happened. Nobody was interested—this was the only contact to know that that had been done. . . . And when we got there, the lady—the receptionist there—she called out here [campus building] and she called to find where was the person who was to be here. And they couldn't find anybody that was supposed to be there to talk with me, so we had to sit there and wait about an hour or two until they found someone to come talk to us. Then when he came in to talk to us, he said that he wasn't interested in the incident. That had no bearing on it . . . and the questions he had asked me had no bearing on the assault or it had no bearing to say whether he was, uhh, displaying, uhh, delinquent tendencies—'cause now that's the first time I heard that phrase used . . . I told them I was willing to sit down and discuss and talk . . . And I explained this to the fellow who did the interview; he said, 'Well, if you want to do that, the only way you can get to sit down and talk with them is to go through the mediation.' I said, 'Well that's fine.' I said, 'We can sit down and I can talk with the other parents.' And I never got any—the next thing I got was a letter telling me I was to go for counseling on Thursday nights, [Her son] and I were to go. I did not go . . . I mean, I was waiting to sit down with the parents to do, you know, but I did not realize the information he was taking was to decide whether he was delinquent, had delinquent tendencies. I mean, if you're fighting, you're fighting. That doesn't mean you're going to be a delinquent. . . . I called and asked them about it, and they said, well there's nothing we can do about that. I said, well, I'm not coming. And I did not go. I was waiting for somebody to come out and get me. . . . If I had had an opportunity to, to sit down and talk about, or if someone would listen to my side of the story. . . . Nobody was interested in what, what—this is their interpretation of what was happening . . . And I was waiting, 'cause I told my niece, you may have to come get me out of jail 'cause I'm not going to be bothered. They could not meet with me to hear my side of the story, so I said, 'I'm not interested in theirs . . . 'Cause I got really offended when he wanted to know who used drugs in my house, how late [her son] was out, because it was in essence telling me that I was a bad parent. All of his questions was, you know, and he couldn't understand when I answered and he—none of my answers seemed to fit like he had pre-, he had already predetermine, you know, that I must, [her son] must be out all times of the night, and everything going on in my house whatsoever. But, and then, then too at the same time, he asked [her son] the same questions after he asked me to see if there was going to be a difference in our stories, you know, as if I was lying. I mean, [her son] told me what he said, you know, and he didn't understand why he was even asked, 'cause some of the things [her son] didn't even know what he was talking about, you know; he's only twelve years old. . . . You have to take the time to listen or to understand where we're coming from.

This respondent spoke at length concerning the fact that the initial risk assessment phase of the program was entered into, not only without her consent, but without her knowledge. She reacted negatively to the presupposition that her son had "delinquent tendencies," or that she was a "bad" parent. We should also note that she fiercely objected to the validity of the original allegations against her child that caused her to be evaluated for the program in the first place. Since the programmatic apparatus begins with a presupposition of consent and the validity of the legal complaint filed against the youth in the first place, there is no facility for a parental point of view such as hers to be heard and where the facts can be legitimately disputed. The respondent went on to review her perspective and the child's perspective on the event that triggered the complaint, involving his "assault" of a fellow female student in school [which both maintain was a clear case of self-defense]. The program was singularly not prepared to meet this parent's real need, which was an opportunity to contextualize the original allegations against her son. Instead she was ordered to go and, as might be expected under the circumstances, balked. She decided to go later at the behest of a family member [who happened to be a mediator for the court] but her resistance to the overall concept remained.

Note also the socio-cultural conflict over the issue of "fighting," what it is and at what level, if any, such activity becomes "delinquent." The African-American socio-cultural tradition allows for self-defense including force as necessitated within the situational context. Therefore, a general Eurocentric designation of "fighting" as wrong and evidence of deviance is an inappropriate framework to employ when deciding whether an African-American child is psychologically dysfunctional. Finally, she objected to the risk assessment methodology as degrading and potentially psychologically damaging to her child, who was asked questions about familial subjects about which he had no prior knowledge.

The second interview was equally informative and enlightening:

Parent: To tell you the truth the problem I had with [her daughter] the program didn't really help.

Daughter: [If she was in charge of the program] I would, like, I wouldn't sit there and say like, I wouldn't give as many speeches. I mean, kids don't listen to speeches. I mean, they hear enough from their parents so they don't really need speeches. . . . They just sat there and talked about— actually I can't remember. They just sat there going on and on—the main guy, I can't remember his name was, kept going on and on and on.

Parent: They just sent a letter saying if you didn't participate in this program, you could spend time in jail and/or have a three-hundred dollar fine.

These two participants go on to relate a generally positive experience. Yet, we still have the problem of the coercive element of programmatic involvement and the feeling that the program counselors are simply not "listening."

The fifth piece of documentation was an article written collectively by many of the principals involved the program. The most striking aspect of this scholarship was the fact that it ignored aspects of white supremacy (Welsing, 1991) entirely as a possible explanatory variable. The authors cite the work of Lockhart et al. (1990) suggesting enormous socio-cultural disparities in the likelihood of arrest, the type of crime charged, the length of sentence and percentage of time served before parole, and the likelihood of conviction.

Consequently, African-Americans are more likely to be in the pipeline for the program. They are also more likely to be simultaneously encountering difficulties in the total spectrum of "people activity," (Welsing, 1991) especially the educational system (Glasgow 1980; Jeffers, 1967; Ladner 1971; Zollar 1985; Ogbu 1974; Rist 1973; Rosenfeld 1971; Silverstein and Krate 1975; Williams 1981).

The psychologists themselves acknowledged disproportionate "difficulties" for African-Americans in school retention rates. This necessarily leads, within the context of the program's calculation of risk factors, to African-Americans' association with relatively high levels of "dysfunctionality." They are then given the maximum level of Eurocentric social intervention. This intervention, in the sense that it does not recognize the fundamental socioeconomic and cultural structures underlying African-American problems, simply papers them over, attributing them to the subjects themselves and to their shortcomings. This negative evaluation of the selfhood of those who are actually "victims," becomes a new oppressive psychological structure that reinforces negative self-evaluations on the part of the subjects, encouraging increasing degrees of "dysfunctionality," and replicating the problems.

In this paper I also found some of the information I had been seeking on risk assessment. The program data were compiled from results of surveys that program entrants had to fill out when they were initially referred. Nixon, who was responsible for risk assessment, compiled the data and a graduate assistant coded them for input and evaluation by computer. The risk assessment measure was a compendium of demographic characteristics, the age at first court referral, the seriousness of the offense, the degree of parental supervision, the level of school "functioning," the "adequacy" of peer groups, the degree of familial alcohol and drug use, and the level of "criminal involvement" in the family. Lack of clarity in the measurement variables was evident. Although the composite scale was designed as a quantitative and objective measure, many of the indicators were subjective and qualitative in character. Who makes the assessment of the "adequacy" of one's peer group and how? Likewise what is school "functionality?" What counts as familial supervision? Finally, the program's risk assessment was said to be derived from APGAR, a standardized self-reported psychological survey (Smilkstein 1978; Doherty and Baird 1983).

The quantification of these variables made me suspicious. "Seriousness of offense" for example, was ascertained by using an index "derived" from a national survey and adapted to the [Southern state] Juvenile Code (Lockhart et al. 1990). "Parental supervision" was evaluated by "integrating" ratings by both parent and child (assessing curfew times, household responsibilities and their completion, and general knowledge of whereabouts). "Peer group affiliations were assessed by determining age differences in friendships, whether peers identified are in the juvenile court system, and the descriptions of peer group activities. The APGAR examined through five items, five areas of family functioning: Adaptability, Partnership, Growth, Affection, and Resolve. It consisted of closed ended questions with three possible responses along the continuum from "hardly ever" to "some of the time" to "almost always." A score of 0 to 3 represented severe "dysfunctionality," 4 to 6 moderate "dysfunctionality" and 7 to 10 "functionality." There were significant statistical associations between these variables, evidence, I believed, of the socio-cultural confounding I noted earlier.

In addition to the quantification problems, there were the problems generally associated with the fact that the data were collected using the classical interview format. I asked as Cicourel (1982) asked whether this approach captured "the daily life, conditions, opinion, values, attitudes, and knowledge base of those being studied as expressed in their natural habitat." And like he, I felt that one could only understand respondent utterances as employed and intended by users within the socially organized context of the collective and within the relationship between the assessor and the respondent. Without considering the collectively defined experience of African-Americans, one had no contextual basis for interpreting responses to particular questions involving area relevant to the respondent's life circumstances (Cicourel, 1967). In cases where the quantity of shared socio-cultural values is low and the fear of strangers is high, a standardized questionnaire and interview approach is unreliable. New methodological approaches are necessary (Benney and Hughes 1956). This is because the validity of the event of intercultural communication is contingent upon shared meanings (Briggs 1983, 1984; Frake 1964, 1977), a point I was later to come back to in my analysis of what was occurring within the site.

I also made a mental note to do some investigation of the family concept as applied in the program. It was clear to me, upon reading this material, that family was a very traditional notion from which the "deviance" of the participants was being judged. This affected the entire program as it revealed a misunderstanding of the dominant characteristics of the African-American family, which is characterized by extended kin units (Webber 1978; Sobel 1979; Aschenbrenner 1975; Jarrett 1992a, 1992b; Sullivan 1985; Valentine 1978; Anderson 1990; Burton 1991; Clark 1983; Hannerz 1969; Holloman and Lewis 1978; Liebow 1967; Martin and Martin 1978).

Slavery blurred these blood lines, but led to the establishment of a functionally-defined family line associating large collectives of biologically unrelated African-Americans into larger social kinship ties (Gutman 1976). This resulted in networks of extended "fictive" kin ties (Stack 1974). Such ties must be considered in evaluating both the constituency of the African-American family and its "adequacy" (Reed 1988).

THE "PERSONNEL" DIMENSION

The second major event preceding my formal observation of the program involved my attendance at the weekly meeting of program counselors, undergraduate assistants, and principal investigators at which, I was to discover, future programmatic plans were made and conclusions were drawn concerning the successes and/or failures from the preceding week's therapy sessions. En route to this session, I ran into Dr. Wind who shared with me the "good news" that the program was likely to be expanded to include a component on family budgeting designed by Dr. "M." of another department. Her "box budget" model would teach the participants to prioritize their expenditures in the direction of paying bills and saving. I could readily see how the perceived needs of the "dysfunctional" family unit steadily increased, necessitating greater planning for more extensive penetration into the family affairs. The addition of this component was, according to him, the subject of a federal grant proposal which would provide funds over and beyond the state funding the program already had. He noted the effect the additional resources would have on the capability of funding assistantships, undergraduate work-study employment, and on the expanding role of the counselors as "advocates" for the families which was his standard name for the role of the staff members.

In the actual meeting, the primary issue was the arrival of three undergraduates [via departmental independent study courses] and a graduate student and what their respective roles would be in the program. The meeting was initially chaired by Dr. Wind, but was alternately helmed by "Marsha" and Dr. Quaser. Marsha asked the undergraduates to give a description of what interested them about this program and whether their preferred focus was quantitative research or counseling. One student had developed an interest in counseling as a result of her experiences in dealing with the care of the sick. Another thought it would be "neat to learn" since her mother had always been involved in social work of some variety. Despite considerable prompting and cuing by Marsha, the students expressed considerable reluctance to enter graduate programs in the field. Marsha responded by suggesting that experience in the program could give one a competitive edge in the application process. Again, the program was being framed in terms of its potential benefit within the context of academia. This occurred despite the assertions by the undergraduates that they possessed some sympathetic or empathetic interest in the care of others. I noted this discrepancy as a vital part of the socialization process for incoming program staff.

Considerable discussion was given to the issue of the effect of these student "transients" on the therapy process and whether that would destabilize the environment. I was specifically included, though not mentioned by name in this debate. The conclusion was that my presence would not be obtrusive, as I would not be engaged in video or tape recording of proceedings. A second undergraduate student was "cleared" when it was found that she would stay involved with program even after the end of her course requirements.

The graduate student arrived under the pretext of taking a more substantive role in the administration of the program and was to be trained for that.

This still left the problem of "what to do" with the undergraduate students, since they needed an unspecified number of hours of labor to meet the requirements for their study. Dr. Quaser asked Marsha whether or not she could use any assistant in compiling quantitative data for the research project, to which she responded negatively. There was another student already well trained for the task, and the research was not of particular interest to the students. One of the students had been around for a few weeks and was asked to summarize her experiences in a manner that might offer insight on potential activities for her coursemates.

Her response to this request abruptly changed the tone of the meeting from informal to more structured and less collegial. She stated that she could only describe her work in the program as "babysitting" and that she would prefer not to do that. Asked to elaborate, she pointed out that two siblings of program participants had no supervision and that she had been unceremoniously given the responsibility for looking after them during the separated sessions for parents and youth. To these two siblings were added two other youth who were actually program participants, but were deemed too young to participate with the other youth in the formal youth session. I jotted down a note to remind myself of the manner in which this problem was approached. Clearly, the presence of very young children is inconsistent with the design of the therapy. Yet rather than pursuing the judicial angle to ask why such youth were prematurely referred, the task of the staff was seen as making provision for the two youth using the same course materials. This met the objective of not contradicting the internal logic of the program and of assigning tasks to the undergraduates. It also facilitated expediency since a social work graduate student who had previously committed to fulfill the role of working with the very young offenders was now unlikely to be available because of a scheduling conflict and the "show had to go on." The conclusions were that some "babysitting" work for siblings of participants was inevitable, but more importantly, that the primary task of the undergraduates would be to provide a "mini-program" for the two "first offenders" that were excluded by age from the group. Immediately, the students "tapped" pointed out that they were unfamiliar with the program. They were told that they would later receive a copy of the program manual [which was available around five p.m.] to read and that they would then be ready to communicate the same concepts to the younger children in session at six-thirty.

What struck me was the manner in which the delicate psychological treatment of the very young was turned over to inexperienced undergraduates. The latter, largely uninformed about the program, could only commit to being around for a few weeks. They had no direct supervision since the rest of the counselors would be in session, yet they were given this serious responsibility. And all of this on the faith that they would gain complete programmatic understanding by reading a text in a single, two hour period. Inordinate faith was placed in either the capabilities of the students or in the documentary power of the text. Dr. Wind's willingness to "shower" me with documentary material and articles concerning the program suggested the latter. Moreover, this was all done without the presence of Dee, the staff head, who would have to rely on secondhand knowledge to integrate them into the scene.

The undergraduate student who had attended the preceding weeks' sessions described the program as prone to chaos, particularly in the relation of incidents like one participant's allegation of sexual abuse in the family, suicide threats, and abrupt departure from the session. It was clear to me, based upon the tentativeness of the principal investigators, that I had now become aware of privileged information, evidenced by the perennial question "can we talk about this, is this, this is supervision?", posed in this case by Dr. Quaser. That is to say, I had come into knowledge of matters that officials within the program sought to keep confidential. I had learned that supervision was a term used to denote closed discussions between counselors and faculty members concerning "clients" in the formal family therapy program. Clients are defined within the first offenders program as being the individual defined as a first offender and his or her immediate family members. In the first offenders program however, the term was a cover for any piece of information that was sensitive to the integrity of the image of the program and was usually invoked in discourse in an interrogative form when there was a question as to whether or not all within the room were legitimate "insiders." The lack of a direct response was a signal that it was "okay" to talk about the issue. Any direct response, usually a simple declarative assertion of "Yes, supervision" implied that no further discussion was appropriate and that the matter should be dealt with behind closed doors. Important to me here was the fact that the undergraduate, not yet an "insider" disregarded the conversational clues and kept talking about the problems associated with "babysitting" and "teenagers talkin' 'bout cuttin' people," in front of me, much to the chagrin of the principal investigators.

At this point I also became aware of a growing preponderance of Euro-American females involved in the psychological treatment of a disproportionately African-American male group, a problem that had gender, as well as race-referent socio-cultural consequences. All three of the undergraduate students and two of the counselors were Euro-American females. Both of the principal investigators were Euro-American males. I only encountered three African-Americans involved in the program, Kirk, Geraldine, and Linda, all counselors, a staff operational ratio of two to one in gender terms in favor of women and three and a half to one in socio-cultural terms in favor of Euro-Americans.

Next, the staff meeting went back to familiarizing the undergraduates with the program. The presentation was directly along the lines of the textual documentation that I had read. Several points did get clarified, however. First, the concept of risk assessment was explicitly defined as a quantitative survey giving researchers data to compile a subjective risk profile. The latter was explicitly stated, in turn, to be a measure of the risk of getting involved in criminality. The judicial principle of "innocent until proven guilty" had been turned on its head by the judicial system feeding the program clients. Individuals referred to the program had, in effect, been found guilty of a tendency towards or desire for future criminality and were being "punished" by "involuntary and voluntary" legal attendance requirements until they had completed the program. More attention was also given to the relative newness of the merger of the family program and the first offenders program and the discontinuity this switch in midstream engendered. This problem was, in the opinion of the principals, overcome by providing for continuity in personnel throughout the twelve week period, explaining the concern with too many "transients."

As Dr. Wind continued, he became conscious of a number of additional needs among them the need for a publication and centralized database of activities for participating parents to assist them in "getting their youth out of the house." There was a hypothesized causal link in the minds of the program staff between the presence of the youth at home during the majority of the day and their alleged propensity towards "criminality." In reality this constituted an unproved assertion of the pseudo-Biblical principle in which "an idle mind is the devil's handiwork." One of the adult counselors stated "Kids need to be interested in something and working towards it to keep them out of their room" and a program official stated "This is the worst time of the year for kids when they have nothing to do" Herein then, lies another assumption about program kids, that they are bored and as a result turn to "criminality" for amusement and activity. Academic tutoring was proposed, but seen as inadequate given the low level of summer school enrollment among the youth in the program. The staff decided to undertake the responsibility of linking parents with "art things" and other community activities to achieve the stated goal, with the undergraduates performing the task of researching and writing the text. They were also required to write end-of-term research papers on what they had experienced in the program.

Getting back to a more substantive manner, a graduate student named Linda came to the meeting to find out her role, which she had been told was to be extensive. Another piece of "privileged" information was broached when Dr. Wind stated," Oh, you're the one that's going to take over the program for Dee." This was corroborated by the statements of Dr. Wind and "Nixon," the risk assessor. It caught Linda somewhat unaware since she had not been given a specific delineation of her responsibilities. She was told to observe in such a manner as to "take over" in fact, to serve as a "spare" counselor in one or more of the groups. She stated that her background was in counseling so she would be well suited for such a role.

Finally, Dr. Wind raised the question of when the next risk assessments would be, since he thought it might be useful to have Linda and possibly me observe. Nixon dismissed the idea of such an external intrusion, stating that it would be destructive to the activity. He stated that although that week's assessment sessions would be on Thursday, he could not guarantee more. It seems that the city-county combined government was commandeering the facility normally used for the assessment interviews and Nixon did not know whether this purpose would permanently preclude use of the site. My next step was to meet with Dee, concerning any additional parameters of my involvement in the program and the site. Dee seemed to counter my preliminary thesis about the motivations for the program in her own description of its origins. She stated that she had been primarily responsible for the textual representation of the program. She had been involved in the "cycle" preceding the one I would be observing and had felt that the program was too culturally exclusive and bore little relevance for the constituency it sought to serve. For example, she stated that it was her initiative to include African-Americans in the program's audiovisual materials. The program had been presented to me as the product of the principal investigators. Dee on the other hand, took primary authorship for herself. During the course of our conversation, we were interrupted by Dr. Wind, and later she reproduced for my benefit the substance of that communication. Specifically, a graduate committee had refused to accept her involvement in the program as her practicum for the degree. She explained that she had had a prior practicum which did not work out and by her own admission, left her psychologically distressed and drained. Since her untimely departure from that program, she had been the victim of departmental rumors concerning her degree of maturity and capacity and whether she could handle the program. These concerns were compounded when the assistantship she had enjoyed as a function of the program was slated for possible removal, a fate that would endanger her academic career. Linda, who I made mention of earlier, was sent as that potential "replacement," unbeknownst to Dee, and I could tell the prospect of removal gave her great pain. I thought this important because it suggested how an individual who actually cared about the sympathetic aspects of the program could gradually be removed. Moreover, this situation of uncertainty and insecurity may have to some degree, affected her ability to administer the program as well as she might. She offered to facilitate any meetings that I would like to have with the group counselors as well as to arrange any research I would like to do with the "subjects" out of the parameters of the program. We agreed that I should wait until the first observation to determine what my programmatic needs would be. It was Dee who allowed me to introduce myself to the group, a matter that was to have repercussions in later sessions in terms of my relationship with the rest of the staff.

PRELIMINARY CONCLUSIONS: IMPLEMENTING THERAPY

I had managed, by virtue of these initial meetings and a careful review of the supporting documentary materials, to isolate the essential elements of a "mind-space" as it had been constructed in this specific instance by the staff and the principal investigators. First, contact by a child with the law was deemed to be illustrative of a larger complex of familial "dysfunctionality." This was established by the identification of corresponding subjective risk profile characteristics. These characteristics, in turn, were associated with certain levels of risk for future criminality on the part of the youth. As such, these factors would presumably have been the target for psychotherapeutic intervention. Paradoxically, they were not. Instead, the family was to be "psycho-educated" and normalized. Poor results on the quantitative risk assessment were assumed to point to poor psychological adjustment on the part of the youth and their respective families.

Second, the knowledge bases of program participants were properly treated as artifacts of the "mind-space" field, as consequences of the assumed "dysfunctionality" rather than as potential sources of counter-explanation or epistemological and ontological critiques of that diagnosis.

Third, the interface, or conduit by which program participants come to be such was also to be viewed as an incidental consequence of familial pathology.

Fourth, the socio-cultural context that facilitated the development of the theory giving rise to the program was viewed as transparent to the process of implementation or, in extreme moments, as nonexistent. As such, the program could be executed by anyone without due training to anyone regardless of demographic discontinuities.

Fifth, "mind-space" as a realm of one's or a group's complete conscious immersion into data was perceived as wholly quantitative. Each virtual reality moment was believed to be mapped onto a continuum of numbers representing definite levels of "dysfunctionality." In positivistic spirit, these unique moments were seen as ordered from zero towards positive infinity with each moment tending towards the next, higher level of pathology.

Sixth, families existed in this "mind-space" as collective entities with the psychotherapeutic diagnoses of each and every member conceived as amalgamated into a larger entity that yet retained the individual deviant characteristics of its component parts.

And lastly, seventh, self-reflection and hermeneutics violated the rules of this "mind-space." As such, the sympathetic, empathetic, and other emotive modes of human expression were to be viewed as either interfering with the "objective" practice of psychotherapy or as illegitimate sources for personal or collective knowledge claims.

HYPOTHESIS FOR POTENTIAL THERAPEUTIC ERRORS

There are several flaws in this "mind-space" as seen from the multicultural psychological perspective. Disregarding the subjective character of the therapist effectively forecloses the examination or re-articulation of his or her preferred cultural and cognitive styles. The standardized nature of the program curriculum prevents both the consideration and incorporation of clients' socio-cultural origins as foundations for psychological readjustment and the promotion of multiple strategic approaches to the resolution of familial problems. The only concordance of this formulation of "mind-space" with the multicultural view involves their joint advocacy of the primary and determinant role of the clients as the agent of psychological self-development.

Similar difficulties are encountered when critiquing this "mind-space" vision from an Africentric socio-psychological perspective. The program begins by violating the fundamental principle that psychotherapeutic theory and methodology involving African-American patients must take into account their experiential reality. Observational and phenomenological cause and effect sequences, heralded by the African-American psychologists as sources of explanations, are rendered imperceptible and supplanted by presuppositions of "dysfunctionality" suggested by quantitative methodology. Clearly, the vantage point of strength and endurance which an Africentric socio-psychological worldview prioritizes as the lens through which patients should be encouraged to "see" their experiences vanishes. The theoretical notion of "dysfunctionality" has as its corollary weakness and the need for psychological retooling. Finally, intuitive truth and consensual validation are expressly proscribed as sources of evidence since they have a hermeneutical and emotive derivation.

In addition, an Africa-centered psychological approach would object to the a posteriori nature of the program, recommending instead holistic health and preventive psychological and social care. More critical to an Africa-centered psychologist would be the participants' competing narratives and knowledge claims, since the latter constitute the primordial cause in this type of psychological inquiry. Africa-centered therapy would also necessitate incursion, by the counselor, into the collective social life of the family to help in ameliorating the social, economic, and/or political pressures which effect their quality of life, and thereby, mental fitness.

Chapter Three

Simulation

"Virtual reality" is a computer-generated simulation of reality and the term is popularly considered to applicable to any phenomenon having a similar quality of appearing to be "real," yet lacking empirical reality. To the extent that the practitioners in the program we are examining, created a unique "mind-space" for themselves concerning the meaning of therapeutic events, the entire therapy session itself could be understood as being a collectively induced moment of "virtual reality." The presumed "dysfunctionality" of the subjects must be "simulated" by the sessions in order to maintain the cognitive disposition of the therapists. Dissonance created by the "clients," positing their own worldviews constitute "shocks" to this closed intellectual system and are systematically rationalized. This is analogous to the techniques of "artificial intelligence" computer programming which endeavors towards perpetual refinement of the mathematics and algorithms of simulation. As the models get "better," so does the perceptual, if not actual line blur between the simulated reality and the world of empiricism. Yet "virtual reality" can come up against a logical philosophical, or perhaps more to the point, "metaphysical" barrier.

To the extent that the uniqueness of humanity is connected to variables like "chance" or "fate" or "divine will," any calculated emulation of human life will fail. Likewise, any objective psychological model not ultimately grounded in the lived experience of those who are deemed subject to it, will fail. The fallacy with the application of deterministic modeling in psychotherapeutic practice is that human beings react in ways not so predictable and have the capacity for a non-intuitive reflection upon and reaction to stimuli. Whatever the theory was, inevitably must bow to the reality of the psychotherapeutic moment. In the context where there is a clash of epistemological and ontological understandings between the therapist and "patient," this necessary genuflection is likely to come as result of a severe body blow to the intellectual ego and to one's canonical paradigms.

As one may expect, the "virtual reality" created within the program falls short in its capacity for anticipating and assimilating the range of participant responses to the curriculum. Some of the most debilitating moments within the program for staff members are those in which participants do not respond according to expectations. While the collective ontological and epistemological orientation of the principal investigators facilitates an a posteriori rationalization of such events, the latter does not help at the site of the actual social interaction itself. Frequently, the staff is left in the sessions as in life with theoretical improvisation, a kind of symbolic jujitsu forced upon them by the patients and their validity claims for counter-knowledge. These moments of improvisational narrative occur of course, with reference to and with an attempt to maintain the integrity of the aforementioned theoretical constraints. In practical terms, they integrate the unanticipated responses into the program as if they were.

This situation would be analogous to a ship's captain who could not bring himself or herself to believe that their ship was in the process of sinking. Any irrefutable evidence that there was in fact, a break in the bulkhead would have to be reconciled with this theoretical position. Imagine that the captain could characterize the break as a natural occurrence, having the effect of balancing the pressure within the vessel, and thus, facilitating and not truncating the voyage.

THE ENVIRONMENTAL CONTEXT OF THE PROGRAM

The role of the participants in the program could be said to have been reflected in the accommodations provided to them upon their arrival. The initial meetings with families when they arrived were held in a child and family development kindergarten classroom (with all the trimmings). There were an insufficient number of regular-sized chairs for the attending families. They had to either retrieve some on their own, rely on Dee or I to bring them some, or resign themselves to the "kiddie" seats. The adult chairs, should the parents have decided to retrieve their own, were located down a hall, around a corner, down some stairs, and in the space formed between those stairs and the floor. In fact, the families often had trouble just trying to get into the buildings where the respective sessions were held. The doors of the child development facility and the bridge connecting it to the clinic were locked by the maintenance staff at five p.m; the sessions began at six-thirty. Dee and I often became the runners, who leapt up at the sound of the knock, figured out which door the sound had emanated from, and then opened it.

At the end of each initial congregation of participants, the parents and youth were split up. The separate sessions were held in two different rooms in the clinic. Participants had to go in the direction of the aforementioned chairs, up a flight of stairs, through a resource room, and through a door. Then they had to make a left turn, a right turn, and then walk across the main waiting room of the clinic. The parents' journey ended here, as one of the therapy rooms on this main floor was used for their sessions. The youth had to ascend yet another flight of stairs to their meeting area. Each week, at the end of the separate parent and youth sessions, both groups had to make the return trip. Between the sessions, there was a snack period in which participants could indulge in refreshments.

The whole ritual of a "homeroom" period with one common instructor and then separate "classrooms" for different periods with different instructors, a "recess" or "snack" period, and then a return to "homeroom" for more generalized instruction with the "homeroom" instructor bore a disturbing resemblance to my routine in secondary school, an analogy made even more palpable by the juvenile decorum that surrounded us.

At this first session there were a considerable number of absentees, based upon the staff's preliminary estimate that there would be twelve families. There were nine members, although they were often missing certain key family members. The youth balance was skewed in the direction of African-American females rather than males. I wondered if such a demographic configuration had been adequately considered in the development of the counseling system. Missing also was Dan, one of the youth counselors. A myriad of new people had to be introduced to the families including the two entering undergraduates and myself. I presented myself as a participant-observer in slightly less than formal language and sat down. Dee told the group that they could express any reservations that they felt about the increased number of unfamiliar people and that an effort would then be made to address their concerns. The parents and youth barely had time to sit down before they were whisked away to their respective group settings. I was introduced to Geraldine, the African-American female counselor and followed her to the site of the youth session.

RUNNING THE PROGRAM: LET THE THERAPY BEGIN

The topics for the evening were feelings, friendship, and "needs." The supervisors of the session were Geraldine and Brooke [an undergraduate].

Questions were raised as to what made the youth feel good or bad about
themselves, about how they were feeling that particular day, as well as about
their respective friendships and the role the latter played in the development
of their feelings. Finally certain needs were itemized and some delineation
of why they were important was made. The primary mode of interaction
involved Geraldine's introduction of questions from the manual. It usually
began with her relation of her own experiences with the relevant subject matter, followed by [with some prodding on the staff's part] statements from the
youth participants. This prodding proved to be a most difficult task, as few
of the participants got involved in the discussion. In fact, on two or three occasions, Geraldine, the African-American female counselor, turned to me to
answer the question and, hopefully, to drive some interaction. Several of the
youth fidgeted in their seats, one became preoccupied with her "Teddy Rux-
pin" [named Brittany and considered one of her best "friends"], and another
refused to participate at all.

At one point, Brooke, a Euro-American female undergraduate expressed
frustration at what she saw as the lack of initiative on the part of the group.
This culminated with her statement that "You people oughta read!" I'm
sure she did not know the connotation that "you people" has for African-
Americans, but after this statement, the session was, in essence, "dead in the
water." The proverbial icing was put on the cake when one student pointed
out that she did not like being at the site because "it [forced participation in
the program] makes me feel like there's something wrong with me." The
counselor attempted to console this individual by stating that the program
did not assume that there was "something wrong with her" but rather, that it
was designed to address her "past mistake(s)." This statement illustrated the
young woman's initial concern. Since many of this cycle's youth came into
the program via judicial proceedings for "truancy," Most of them probably
did not consider their first offense as a mistake.

One point came up during the discussion (which I assumed would be a
primary focus of the therapy [as a result of the reliance upon the text-based
program]) but which was ignored in the actual session. There was an interlude
in which the youth watched a set of movie excerpts [which they had seen the
preceding week] that were supposed to illustrate a variety of feelings and
responses to them. During one scene from "Boyz N' The Hood," the African-American main character has a gun drawn on him at point blank range.
In another, he has to decide whether or not to join his friends in a quest for
revenge. During the showing of this piece, I heard comments like "He's a
punk." Presumably, this referred to the main character's unwillingness to
engage his enemies through material force. No comment was made by the
counselors upon these responses. In discussion concerning another scene, an

excerpt from "Juice" where the major character's girlfriend is seen getting into the car with another African-American male. The general consensus among the youth was that, in the defense of his honor, he should have materially confronted both the woman and the man. His failure to do so constituted "weakness." The counselor spent the next several minutes before the session was called to a halt trying to illustrate the fact that such a confrontation may not have been the best option under the circumstances, but to no avail.

SYNTAX ERROR

In computer terminology, a "syntax error" might be simplistically described as a grammatical or diction error in programming which leads to the inability of a compiler to "read" or understand a particular line or set of lines of code. Essentially, this is a communication breakdown between the programmer and the computer. Following our "simulation" analogy, one can describe the errors beginning to show in the operation of the program as "syntax errors" in which the presumptions of the program and its therapy staff about reality are not being "computed" by the subjects who are supposed to process them.

One can draw several conclusions from these interchanges. One, was the fact that the program had not considered the role of disrespect as a trigger for collective or individual self-defense within the African-American self-esteem structure and the degree to which it affects the evaluation of behavioral and communicative responses. Responses to the challenge of disrespect do involve public evaluation of one's actions, but it is the style and not the effectiveness of the actions that are judged (Peristiany 1966). Under a common African-American code of honor, a refusal to grant deference amounts to an insult, while accepting another's claim to superiority is tantamount to dishonor. Dishonor is experienced as a failure of the capacity to maintain claims to precedence among peers.

Second, the text-driven approach of the program was impeding its progress. There was not sufficient flexibility to address topics as they arose. This was a function of the research imperative always lurking being the scene, since only by completing the program on time and according to the letter of the law could one be sure that the data for the study met Eurocentric standards of reliability, validity, replicability and generalizability.

[L], the young African-American woman who refused to participate, first turned around in the opposite direction to show her displeasure and finally walked out of the session . This was not helped by the fact that Geraldine mispronounced her name on three separate occasions. Each mispronunciation seeming to strike her like an arrow, her face becoming more contorted with each occurrence. I later saw her standing on the bridge between the child development center and the clinic staring aimlessly into space. What I found even more disturbing was the fact that only Geraldine [among the staff] and myself tried to get her to go to the joint snack session after the youth meeting; everyone else walked right by. This was particularly stressful to me because she was the youth who had alleged sexual abuse, allegations which I felt were taken far too lightly at first by the program staff but more seriously by school, religious, and human service agencies. At some point, she did rejoin the group and interact with Geraldine and the large collective, but would not interact with Brooke. I later learned that Brooke had previously betrayed her confidence by relaying a confidential letter to the program staff.

THE BEST MISLAID PLANS

The youth session was followed, after snack, with the collective session. Central in this discussion, led by Dee, was the need to use "I" messages rather than "you" messages in communicating desires from parents to children and vice versa. There was also attention given to the need to explain why requests were being made. Considerable dissonance was apparent in the group among parents at this point and I believe it had distinct socio-cultural origins.

As I was mulling over this, I took in a sight that was to be replayed over and over in my mind, and that brought to the forefront the need for socio-cultural training for some of the staff. Brooke was complimenting an African-American youth on the beauty of her dreadlocks and rubbing through them. Immediately I thought of the historical southern "white" male and female practice of "rubbing the heads" or "feeling the hair" of African-American children with "dreads" or other socio-culturally bound styles out of curiosity or novelty in the way that one might pet a dog.

In a few minutes more, the discussion turned into a nightmare for the counselors. The rigidity of the text-based program strategy and discussion format excluded external social institutions as potential causes or explanations for familial problems. The introduction of just such a factor by one disgruntled parent brought the flood. Dee had noticed some degree of antagonism on the part of several of the parents and voiced her concern. One mother responded by stating that she was indeed angry about her own presence there since, she maintained, she had no business being there. She went on to clarify her feeling that she "was in trouble for being [there]" and that she had begun to think that it was "her fault." Resisting in her own mind and orally such an idea she pointed out that her son had been judicially prosecuted for "truancy." She countered that in actuality, he had not been "truant" but that the school had purposely ignored her notification that her son had had to have an extended stay in the hospital. She had tried to bring his homework to him in the hospital, but the school had been either incapable or unwilling to yield to her request. This was fit into a personal collage of historical negative relationships with the school, which she identified. At this point, there was a supporting statement made by one of the youth that "dey jus' prejudice' anyway," suggesting a communal knowledge base that the school had problems with African-American parents and children. According to the mother's account, she exemplified the model of the good parent, attending all of the "special education" conferences, PTAs, and the like, but still received neither assistance nor respect. These comments struck a particularly resonant tone for me, since I had recently been involved in trying to extricate a woman's three "dysfunctional" children from the clutches of special education programs in another state. To the program counselors such an assertion was not only to be questioned in terms of validity, but constituted a challenge to the legitimacy of the program itself. Dee tried unsuccessfully to channel the anger of the mother back into the text-based lesson for the day on "I" messages. Geraldine, in fact, leaned over to Linda and said "She [Dee] is not ready for this" Not ready here, refers to the fact that the mother was making a knowledge claim as to the basis for her involvement in the program and the root of her difficulties that related neither to the topic of the moment nor to the supposition of the program that dysfunctionality indeed resided within the program's families.

The mother then turned from the educational system to the judicial system, stating that the judge had threatened to jail her if she did not attend the program and that he had done so in a snide manner. She quoted him as stating that "he didn't care whether the program was beneficial or not, or whether they [the parents] had transportation to get to the program, but that they would have to attend or both they and their children would be jailed." This destroyed any illusion that this was a voluntary program. I called this the "bench warrant" episode because she quoted the judge as calling out orally "Bench warrant!" for each parent that was not present at the required judicial proceedings for their youth. Many parents joined the chorus of "Amens!" at this point since they had experienced the same treatment with the same judge. Floundering, Dee tried to get back to the manual, processing anger via the "I" message material. The second time, she was undermined by Geraldine who tried to insinuate that the parent's particular structural difficulties might have been due to her own attitude and to the labeling of the mother's child as a "problem."

The parent became totally defensive at this point, stating unequivocally that she had no problem with her children in terms of communication or otherwise and reiterating her stories of maltreatment. The resolution after a few more minutes of cross conversation and dissension in the group was that the matter would be held over for about four weeks when a representative from the school system would be present to answer such concerns. Dee then regained control of the rostrum and went back to her musings about the "I" messages and the negative sensations associated with feeling ' controlled," but by this time the session, like the youth session before it, was for all practical purposes at a conclusion. The keynoting parent left swiftly at the end of the session. She seemed disgruntled about the manner in which her concerns and feelings were dealt with.

I felt a mixture of so many strong emotions after this event that I underwent a weeklong personal debriefing session with anyone who would listen so I could try to purge myself before my next onslaught. With my roommate, program mentor, and my then-fiancée, I vented my shock, disgust, anger, and frustration with the program for being so insensitive, inflexible and socio-culturally unaware. Like some type of inverted Socratic figure, I questioned my own motives, remembering that I had a commitment to help African-American people before becoming involved in the program, but had approached the counseling clinic activities in ignorance. I spent many sleepless hours debating how I might manage a participant-observer role that was increasingly becoming one of unpaid consultant for the staff rather than researcher. The results had already gone beyond the traditional boundaries of constructive criticism and towards a more thoroughgoing epistemological critique. After my "debriefing" , I had learned how good it was to get away from the site for a while and be myself. Then I could go back in with a list of questions to see how the staff "saw" what I had seen, and whether they had felt what I had felt in observing these phenomena.

GHOST IN THE MACHINE

The rock band The Police had an album in 1983 entitled "Ghost in the Machine." One of the singles from this album was entitled "Sprits in the Material World." Both the song and the album related generally to the systems view of society and how it atomizes and commodifies human life. Pardoxically, that commodification only reveals the essential non-materialistic needs of humanity which are rooted in values like communication, equity, justice, love. These are normally rendered as non-scientific or as "spiritual" values. This is commonly understood to be beyond the pale of most Western disciplines with the exception of theology and philosophy. Yet study after study has reminded us that to the extent that our humanity and our conduct in and concerning society is in whole or in part influenced by this "spiritual" quality, it must be a concern of sociologists. It becomes a concern of psychologists when they are attempting to engage therapy of oppressed populations because oppression is itself largely constituted as a mental perception of deprivation of these spiritual goods.

In our example, we might describe the rigidity of the psychotherapeutic program here, its justificatory theories, and the limitation of its cross-cultural applicability as the "machine." The families in the program thus become ghosts, their empirically realities rendered invisible and/or irrelevant to their "cure."

This chapter illustrates clearly in case after case that the participants' view of "reality" was fundamentally at odds with that of the staff and shows us how difficult it was for the latter when competing knowledge claims were advanced. The program, theoretically speaking, was supposed to effect such a comprehensive sensory "blanket" that participants would treat the simulation as their own. Yet, the program's inattention to external, intervening factors led to a diminishing of its impact on the perception of the subjects. In a metaphorical sense, the three-dimensional headgear of the virtual reality unit had been short-circuited by socio-cultural reality.

The multicultural theoretical perspective suggests to us many of the reasons for the problems identified in this chapter. Specific among these is the lack of acknowledgement on the part of the program of the existence and intrusion of the therapists' cultural and cognitive styles. The disgruntled parent was operating from a collective, communal rhetorical style. In such a formulation, a topic is systematically keynoted through the group, with each member adding his or her spin on the situation to the tapestry of understanding. When there is a competing knowledge claim, that claim is not interpreted as a refutation of what has gone before, but as another piece of valid information that illuminates questions that have been raised.

In the conventional psychological therapists' cognitive style, the key emphasis is on authority. Competing knowledge claims are to be viewed as challenges to authority and as aimed at a transfer of power from the current dominant speaker to a "pretender." Discussion in such a style revolves within the parameters established by the dominant speaker. Clearly, the view of Dee and the rest of the staff concerning the parent "with the problem" was not that the latter was giving additional information, but that she was maliciously impeding progress and the program's ability to reform her supposed dysfunctionality.

An Africentric psychological perspective would focus on the manner in which the competing knowledge claim was presented, that is to say, in terms of a straightforward observational cause and effect sequence. The problem of the parent was seen to stem directly from relationships with the judicial and educational systems in a direct chain of events. The counselors here reverted to the type of mental explanations that an Africentric view seeks to avoid; trying to explain the outburst in terms of individual psychological inadequacies rather than systemic problems. Clearly, consensual validation and the acceptance of people's words as they relate to their own collective experiences were deemed invalid within the program as sources of information. The paradigm of dysfunctionality remained dominant and determinant as the explanation for behavior and response.

An Africa-centered psychological perspective would focus on the discrepancy between the ontological model of the family within the program theory and an African-American model. Within the latter, collective selfhood sits at the focal point of a concentric set of circles beginning with the parents, moving to the elders, the community, the nation, and finally, to the Creator. Each level is sovereign within itself. This means that youth are sovereign over that which is the rightful dominion of youth, collectively defined. The parents' [biological and/or functional] dominion is inclusive of youth's dominion and more extensive. Bargaining for decision-making power takes place among equals at the relevant level. The parents' for example, are subject to other elders such as their own parents. The youth, until the age of maturity, are subject to parent(s). The youth assumes a bargaining position with parents when he or she is able to fulfill all of the collectively required responsibilities of the parent in the society outside of their required assistance. Priority is always given to experiential knowledge. The self is not a Eurocentric independent being, but a collectively nurtured and sustained one. The same programmatic impetus that suggested youth programs would have to be addressed within the familial structure, would have been advised to consider the implications of working within the constraints of that structure. This was an issue that came up repeatedly when dissent arose between the parents and counselors over the relative influence of youth preferences within the parental sphere.

Chapter Four

The Patient as "Object"

We have already seen within our metaphorical reference that psychotherapeutic "head games" have at least two minimum requirements. The first is that a "mind-space" be allocated and defined and objects placed within it that determine the "virtual reality" to be experienced by the "patient." To this realm is added repeated session simulation that attempt to reinforce a notion of dependence on the "system" and of personal responsibility for one's alleged psychological problems. The result of the interaction of the definition of a "mind-space" and the application of "simulation" sessions is that the patients are systematically objectified by the therapist and are taught to objectify themselves. For the therapist, they are the raw mental material in which may be engraved, a la *tabula rasa* the psychotherapeutic enterprise. Similarly, a "cured" patient effective de-contextualizes their experience and becomes beholden to the therapists' view of "reality." The problem here is that the cross-cultural dimension acts as a *prima facie* barrier to the effective assimilation of the Eurocentric psychotherapeutic ideology of the researchers and thus, confounds the "cure." A psychotherapeutic program that is striving to be "cross-cultural" must contend with the likelihood that various individuals will not participate and that their nonparticipation is not indicative of a "resistance to therapy," but rather an unwillingness to allow themselves to be "objectified" within the epistemological frame set up by the therapy. Several examples in this chapter will show the degree to which the program fell woefully short in grappling with this difficulty.

RATIONALIZING FAILURE

At this stage I felt that the staff was adjusting its "fronts" to accommodate my presence. On one hand, the deconstruction of *prima facie* images of the program was positive in that it allowed me to understand previously hidden aspects. But just as these facades were undermined by my growing knowledge of the program and of its intimacies, other facades, more resilient, were being constructed. The erection of these perceptual barriers took the form of political spin doctoring where the staff began to anticipate what they felt may have been negative impressions I had gathered about the program and responded by giving me their alternate definitions of the situation. The evaluation of the week's activities preceding my arrival involved some constructive criticism, but nothing on the scale of the subsequent sessions. All of the activities of the following week were punctuated by negative assessment of occurrences on the part of the staff, measures taken to relieve these problems, and apologies designed to explain the occurrences in light of pragmatic program development.

The first such re-articulation occurred within the weekly evaluation meetings. The first topic was the perennial concern over allocation of the undergraduates' time. It was finally agreed that there was one too many of them working with the program youth. The youth they had been working with were then organized into two groups of two members each supervised respectively by Kathryn and Alecia. There was some initial concern over the reliability of the latter woman since she regularly appeared ten to fifteen minutes late, but the matter was resolved. What was especially interesting about these perennial discussions at this point was the fact that they revealed that the clinical staff harbored the same opinion about undergraduate aides as they did about the actual "clients" themselves with regard to the need to avoid youth "idleness."

The undergraduates also continued their quest to assemble a guide of things-to-do for the parents and Linda offered African-American churches as potential sites for information. They were also assigned the task of assembling an annotated bibliography of references on qualitative research on the subject of "treating" juvenile "delinquency." This was a consequence of the inability of the program's in-house quantitative data to provide insights on the particular problems the program was having and was also a reflection of the fact that my presence as a researcher encouraged the program to begin "thinking" qualitatively.

Linda, despite admitting having no clinical experience, was allocated a case management load of her own involving calling families when they missed a session, evaluating familial attendance, and finally counseling with Marsha or Dan when formal family therapy was required. Some discussion was made concerning the size of the parents group, but the general consensus was that it had not yet grown too unwieldy. Dan, the Euro-American male counselor who was absent the preceding week, took up the situation of [L]. He noted that there had been consultations with the family concerning her allegations of sexual abuse and that this discussion seemed to have had a positive effect on [L]'s behavior, as evidenced by her increased participation in the previous week's sessions. He then noted that he would be absent again a week hence. Marsha said she also would be absent soon.

Dan then reclaimed the floor to speak about the fact that he had been recently consulted on a case in which a program participant had been involved in a second offense and that he had tried to act as an advocate on the side of the youth, stipulating that the behavior was an anomaly for that individual [I later learned that [Q] was the one being referred to]. It seems important to note that when an individual or family was participating "successfully" in the program, they were considered as becoming less dysfunctional. Behavioral difficulties were not programmatic failures but flukes.

Brooke asked whether she could begin bringing gum and/or candies to the youth session as icebreaking elements that would encourage the youth to talk more. Dr. Wind was considerably ambivalent about this because of the fact that participating parents might not have wanted sugar consumption on the part of their children. Marsha voiced a common concern about the influx of new people and observers and the effect that that may have had on the proceedings. My presence was even brought up as a potential contributing factor. Characteristically, the program staff was prone to blame influences external to themselves for shortcomings and/or administrative glitches. An agreement was made to place a moratorium on such outsiders for the next two weeks of the program in order to give the participants the feeling of continuity. Debate went into the realm of scheduling, and whether the upcoming session around a holiday should be cancelled and nonbinding therefore, on participants. The general consensus was that participants would be asked and if a majority were perceived as likely to be absent, the session would be rescheduled. I was asked at this point what, if any preliminary observations I might wish to make concerning the program. I simply asked for the collective staff definition of the previous week's session situation with the disgruntled parents. Several points materialized in response to this inquiry. First, a thesis that the keynoting parent was on drugs gained general staff acceptance, explaining away the concern (a common phenomenon as I was to find out in talking with Dee later). Statements were made to the effect that a firm hand had to be used in order to avoid "takin' everyone's time" and to "stay on track." This reiterated my earlier point concerning the extent to which parental behavior not anticipated by the system is viewed with extreme suspicion, as warranting rationalization, and as a unnecessary delay. Incidentally, at the conclusion of the meeting I continued my quest for the "risk assessment" material, but to no avail. Dr. Wind said that he had requested it from Nixon, but had received nothing.

DEE ON THE WARPATH: INSIDER-OUTSIDER VIEWS

I had learned by this week that arriving early for the week's sessions gave me an opportunity to interact with any program staff members who were on hand, particularly Dee who took me under her wing and perceived me as a kindred spirit of sorts in the sense that she, too, was an insider-outsider. I helped move chairs and with preparations, scattering questions as I went and listening to her assessment of the overall status of the program. By "insider-outsider," I mean that Dee appeared to be more and more marginalized over time from the rest of the staff and the principal investigators.

To open up the discourse with her, I would summarize, as accurately as I could remember, the details of the afternoon staff meeting held some hours before. I had a long standing curiosity as to why she never attended those sessions. She initially told me that she had a scheduling conflict, but as she continued she said "I have never been [formally, I assume] asked" and that she didn't need [such a meeting] to evaluate the program, she "feels" when it's right. This was said in what I detected to be a slightly irritated tone, consistent with a developing image of her as slightly "out of the loop." She reminisced at some length about her previous "cycle" role as session facilitator or counselor, which she saw as vastly superior to her role as "head." The latter responsibilities did not give her an opportunity to interact on a personal basis with the parents or the youth, something she identified as very important. She made it unequivocally clear that the joint session the preceding week was a failure. She identified three factors as causal. First there was the presence of a large number of "new" people. She noted this, although she emphasized her flexibility relative to other staff personnel on this point. Second there was the failure of the facilitators [counselors] to take a role in "keynoting" the discussion in the large group. She argued that as a result of this failure the moderator was not as aware of sentiments concerning the presentation. And, three, the arrangement of the space during "snack" which she felt did not afford an opportunity for parents to interact. She did not identify the triggering moment of the parent's concern as a sore point, so I specifically asked for her characterization of the situation, feigning relative ignorance on the actual exchange itself.

With increasing emotion, she stated that she would not "sacrifice the group session for an individual [or an individual family's] concerns." As the disgruntled parents spoke, she felt that she was "losing these other people." Dee maintained that "if you didn't need it [the program], you wouldn't be here," further validating the confidence that the staff and the principal investigators had in the accuracy of the "risk profile." Therefore, the pleas of families for excusal on most grounds were eliminated a priori. Like other staff members, she maintained a perception of the value of an individual client's comments based upon the type of interaction that the individual engages in, rather than the content. The mother's perceived antagonism led to her being labeled as "possibly on drugs," a point of view that was cited by Dee as a general consensus. Furthermore, she seemed genuinely taken aback by any suggestion that the program should address more systemic issues, not strictly within its field of inquiry. Familial structure adequacy is the only legitimate object of concern. She said, "What we can do is make their family structure strong, so that it doesn't collapse." which can be taken as her own personal prejudgment of the present condition of the families. Individuals who bring up counter-explanations are, in fact, "offenders" of a different sort. As Dee plaintively put it, "we were trying to talk about communication, how you communicate with your kids" Clearly, she was peeved that her agenda was scuttled and indicated some fear about a recurrence the upcoming week. In fact, she advanced the hypothesis that the parents who did not wish to attend regularly sought to gain revenge by making everyone else miserable. She cited as evidence for this hypothesis the lack of collaborating testimony or body language on the part of the other parents, in stark contrast to my observation data. She pointed out that such anomalies were to be viewed as a consequence of the effort to develop the logistics pragmatically and that she sought to grapple with the problems by instituting with Dr. Wind a debriefing session to be held immediately after the program.

MORE BUGS IN THE PROGRAM

The next session of the youth group that I attended marked the return of Dan, the undeclared "leader" of the youth group from the staff perspective. I say this because Geraldine arrived late and confined her comments to "piggy-backing" off of Dan's comments and inquiries rather than participating as a full partner. Likewise, Brooke was marginalized, and since Dan had not yet grown accustomed to my role, I managed to avoid center-stage entirely. The only time I entered was during an exercise in which each individual was subject to the relatively unsolicited praise of others in the group and one student insisted that I and the counselors be included.

At the beginning of the session, one student, [M], was leaning to one side on a couch and was apparently sleeping. We later found out that this was due to his long day at his Job Partnership Training Agency program job which was paying him for working and attending school by any measure a positive turn of events. Without initially soliciting this knowledge, however, Dan was left to conclude that [M] was merely being inattentive. What followed was a set of subtle and not so subtle methods Dan tried to gain [M]'s attention. First, he stated that the first positive comment about [M] was that he "had nice eyelids" a reference to his apparent slumber, but one that was out of context given Dan's initial injunction that nothing said about a group member should be a "putdown." He verbally acknowledged that he had violated his own maxim. Shortly thereafter, he hurled a pencil at [M] striking him to encourage him, I presume, to stay awake. This was followed by a request for other session participants to "Kick him!" This could have caused a major disturbance had his request been taken up, as [M] had specifically requested that he be left alone. It was much later in the session when Dan asked and promptly acquired the whole story concerning [M]'s brutal schedule and exhaustion. A psychological session devoted to the inculcation of positive self-image among the "clients" was undermined by a counselor focusing unjustified and inappropriate negative attention upon a single individual, employing even battery to make its point.

Most of the comments concerning group members involved their being "nice," "quiet," or "friendly." What was striking, however, was the extent to which the assessment made by some members of the group concerning others was not "right" in the eyes of the staff. In particular, there was a case in which a young African-American woman identified another's positive characteristic as being "shy." To this assertion, the counselors gave derisive looks and statements of incredulity. The youth deftly defended herself by responding, "that's a good thing. Shy ain't no bad thing" Again, the context suggested that one could take advantage of "quiet space" [uninterrupted floor time] to say anything one considered positive about others, but the reality suggested otherwise. Several youth had to endure painful, lengthy pauses when their name was called, surely exacerbating any lack of self-esteem and self-worth they might have.

An even stranger encounter provided more information about participants' perceptions of the program when a young woman described a young male as "crazy." She quickly followed that, amidst giggles, with a clarification that by "crazy," she meant silly or amusing. The fact that such a clarification would not have been necessary in a context outside of this one, validates the points the youth had made in preceding sessions. One concerned their fears that participation in the program was an indication that there was something mentally wrong with them or that they were dysfunctional. The other concerned their needs to constantly reassure themselves, within the context of group discussions, that they were not "crazy."

The difference in perception I noted in a previous session between the counselors and their "patients" over the issue of whether the youths' initial first offenses were solely the latter's fault was confirmed when Geraldine asserted that one of the positive characteristics of a particular African-American female participant was that "she would not be making mistakes like this again."

The format of this exercise was strange anyway. The point was to say something positive about each member of the group. It was introduced to [M] with the following exchange:

[M]: Well. I'm 'spose ta compliment somebody?

Dan: No. I'm going to compliment you.

[M]: Well den, what I do?

Dan: You jus' listen.

Clearly, [M] has no idea of the relevance of this exercise to anything and is attempting to please the counselor by complying. Dan later complimented [M] after this exchange on just such deference behavior. After this exercise, Dan asked about whether parents said something nice about the youth, to which the majority replied in the negative. [L], the student who did not interact in the previous session but seemed in a better mood this week, maintained that her mother did not say positive things about her. Rather than validating [L]'s point of view, Geraldine disagreed saying, "You probably didn't realize it [something she said] was nice." This was another example of the pattern of channeling any truly dissenting comments and sentiments into the expected paradigmatic responses by reinterpreting or denying them.

Things got even worse when [M] told about his positive job experience and Geraldine suggested that the program he was involved in [which she had attended in younger years] paid well enough to warrant misleading legal authorities to enter it. Specifically she stated, "If your dad makes a lot of money, use your mom [as primary income source, I presume]." A disturbing thought that individuals with so-called "delinquent tendencies," already on the brink of incarceration, would be told to break the law if it was convenient for personal economic gain. Finally, the session closed with a vain attempt to get the youth to define "self-esteem," resulting in a counselor-posited definition and to open discussion between Geraldine and Dan as to session inadequacies and whether they should open up with a video next time. They also concluded that the youth group was becoming too large and unwieldy [with nine people?] Overall, the mood of the group was as dead as the preceding week, with two respondents falling asleep entirely and at least four others manifesting yawns and a state of general disinterest and distraction.

This "deathlike" state was to prove to be relevant for the entire program as the parents' discussion ran well over the fifty minute limitation imposed by the program, its participants not arriving in the joint session until 8:09 p.m. [roughly thirty minutes before the scheduled end of the session]. They still had to have "snack" at that point, effectively truncating the joint session to fifteen minutes.

FROM BOYZ II MEN

To the African-American female youth, Geraldine was a friend and mentor outside of her counselor role. The African-American males had no such mentor. Kirk, the only African-American male counselor, was elsewhere, helping supervise the parental discussions. While Geraldine sat with a group of girls, their attention riveted upon her every word, the boys' discussion moved in an unsupervised negative direction emphasizing the glory of successful illegal behavior. This caused me again to give attention to the effectiveness of the program in terms of the gender and race-referent socio-cultural balances in the staff and with respect to its capacity to grapple with the problems of young African-American males.

STRESSFUL RELAXATION

When the parents did get settled, one of the funniest scenes at the program took place. Dee instructed everyone to close their eyes. Several parents verbally protested "What we 'spose to see?" and "I don't want to sit in the dark!" Laughter, needless to say, ensued on the part of most of the parents. I sensed a major perceptual gap at this point, as Dee thought she was engaging in some sort of realistic psychological relaxation exercise, and the parents thought the program had reached the point of ultimate ridiculousness. She went on to try to get the parents and youth to "think about how they felt [presumably "good"]."

This was followed by a culminating lecture on the principles of parental and youth spheres of "control" and the opposing idea of "working together." "Control" is, roughly, unilateral decision-making. "Working together" is a type of parent-child negotiation. The parents noted that they did not and would not negotiate with their children for access to their rooms, on matters regarding what friends are "acceptable" in their households, and such. Dee responded by suggesting that this was simply an area in which more work had to be done. She reminded the parents that they were raising "future adults."

NOMINAL ASSESSMENT CONTINUED

The session was followed by the first debriefing session. Marsha said that one of the parents had another male child [not in the program] who got into trouble for playing too rough and fighting. The mother explained that this was the result of the tough style of playing that characterized the child's older brothers. She stated that she had no idea what to recommend except family therapy, which she said the mother was willing to attend. None of the group members had any suggestion either and the matter dropped. Clearly, again familial and/or socio-cultural problems beyond the specified parameters of the program were considered unsolvable or fit into the paradigm in a tortured manner. In this case, a male child's predisposition towards roughness translates into familial therapy needs. This despite Marsha's admittance that such a recommendation was made only because there was nothing else to propose. The only counter suggestions were in the area of sports, the perennial resolution path for "troubled" African-American male youth. It was Dee alone who pointed out that roughness was "not always bad" in the face of a group which had already placed it within the category of psychological problem.

The parents' session was lauded for its success in getting people to talk (so much so that the parents were late) and arrangements were made for extra time in the sessions for longer discussions forthcoming on important topics like peer pressure and violence. Dan characterized the youth session as less enthusiastic than desired and restated his and Geraldine's commitment to employ video early in the next session. At this point, the meeting was adjourned.

MISSING SOCIO-CULTURAL DIMENSIONS IN THE EVALUATION PROCESS

I drew a preliminary conclusion at this point that the parental sessions were marginally successful in that the parents had no intention of accepting anything that they did not choose to accept with regard to their parenting practices. Clearly this is my definition of success and not the program's. Similar developments were impeded within the context of the youth group because the participants had been branded as "recovering dysfunctionals" by the legal and psychological system (in front of their families) and as a result, were subjected to more systematic socio-cultural coercion upon their behavior.

The statements about "household democracy" were lost on the ears of the African-American parents. They were then chided and told to work a little harder on mastering the concept. Likewise, the student whose work schedule made him sleepy was diagnosed initially as a "sloucher" and the response was to generate collective disfavor and the commission of battery against him. In each case, one or more "patients" refused to either accept the knowledge claims of the program or to posit their own surrogates. Rather, they psychologically withdrew. Such a withdrawal did not allow the program to operate on that person. They would not become "objects" within the psychotherapeutic process.

The multicultural psychological perspective would emphasize the extent to which the primary difference here was one of cognitive and socio-cultural style as it related to discipline. The program posited that the appropriate disciplinary model was one involving negotiations between supposed equals. The idea was that the mutual consent of the parties would be likely to make the results favorable to both. The parents focused on the need to get the youth to perform tasks that the latter did not wish to perform. It was, in their estimation, impossible to negotiate terms with someone who was not interested in completing the task that was to be the object of negotiation. This was a difference of methodology. Moreover, the program had itself as its highest priority. And it clearly ranked high in the list of priorities for the staff and principal investigators. But it did not rank as high in the minds of the participants, many of whom attended under duress or were experiencing distracting external concerns so great as to warrant their primary focus. The youth who slept was entirely unsympathetic to the "need" of his attention to a program that was being weighed against his capability to earn a wage. The therapist was equally unsympathetic in the opposite direction.

An Africentric psychological perspective would point out the inattention to the experiential reality of the subjects. The parents were merely coming from a parental experience that had been a part of their familial structure for generations. The youth in the example was focusing on the task of employment and wage-earning, not on an after-school psychological class. In each case, the program could not accommodate the perspective of the client. To do so would be to question the epistemological foundations of the program itself which suggests that the subjects should be interested in the process of changing their ways. However, the only reason one would want to change his or her ways is if he or she felt that they were dysfunctional. We have already seen that this was a contested characterization of these families.

The Africa-centered psychological perspective would note the pitting of African collective selfhood against Eurocentric individualist, "democratic" selfhood. In the Eurocentric model it is the adult part of the phrase that is operative, suggesting that a child assumes adulthood incrementally through extension of responsibility and rights by the parent until he or she is mature.

In the Africa-centered approach, the child assumes adulthood as a resultant product of having executed responsibilities and exercised rights delineated by elders as evidence of his or her completion of the appropriate socio-cultural "rites of passage." This view would also note the sheer hypocrisy inherent within a program that is concerned about invalidating the right of physical self-defense while using various means of psychological and in this specific case physical coercion to accomplish its therapeutic objective. It would explain this paradox in terms of the Eurocentric cultural ethos and its focus on its own power. The use of force, in this formulation, is confined to the pursuit of "legitimate," Eurocentric objectives. In this case, those objectives are the psychological proselytizing of an individual. That individual, conversely, is denied by definition the right of defending themselves because of the very notion that the offending party is acting the latter's "best interests" in imposing Eurocentric socio-cultural imperatives.

Chapter Five

Weapons of Mass Distraction

Jorge Luis Borges (1970) theorized about a Library of Babel consisting of volumes with neither title nor author. These volumes were composed of arbitrary collections of symbols, each one a combination of all the possible combinations of the letters of the alphabet. Every possible text is included. Looking for an unwritten, yet specific narrative like one's earthly demise would be impossible. One simply would not know where to begin the search. The act of searching would itself be part of the story. Yet, it seems within the realm of possibility to find those stories which have been written in the past and to use them as indices or "windows" to variations on their respective themes.

Another useful "virtual reality" analog for our purposes is "hypertext." "Hypertext" focuses on cyberspace a storage facility for a simulated literary construct. It begins with the germ of a familiar narrative scenario, known to the user as a consequence of sharing the "author's" world. I place "author" in quotes here, because beyond the initial textual narrative setting the stage, the literary experience is written by the user and the outcomes are to some extent limited only by the computing capacity available and the user's sense of creativity. Many of the most successful microcomputer text adventures like Zork are based on precisely such textual elaboration. The user navigates himself or herself through the textual "world," alternately articulating and rearticulating the narrative. The reader becomes the author. And the narrative systematically becomes less a fixed object or "product" of the author than an alternate or "virtual" reality.

The psychotherapy program I am analyzing is, at its core, an implementation and operationalization of a theoretical research text. The parameters, theories, and objectives are linguistically codified in program documentation.

Initially, the program began by sticking strictly to the text-based format. The counselors, in many cases, literally "read" the curriculum into the reality of the sessions. Over time, the inevitable tension posed by the textual inadequacies as they related to socio-cultural realities led facilitators to begin deviating. This deviance was not systematic, but rather schizophrenic and haphazard. The clients in this newly reconstituted "mind-space" could control the narrative and thereby the cognitive power of the program. In this chapter, we examine the beginning of a collapse in the program. This decline was triggered by the recognition of staff and clients that the textual reality was inadequate, and that new "hypertext" narratives needed to be put forward. This new balance of influence between staff and clients forced the issue of competing socio-cultural styles and knowledge claims to a head.

The title of this chapter stems from the perpetual tension between the text-based aspect of the program and the social interactions that were occurring at the level of its implementation. Thus began a "war of wills" between the clients and the staff as to whether the program would in effect devolve into informality and a discussion among equals or whether it would maintain itself as a "session" directed by superiors. The states were high, and they were not purely communicative. The principal investigators' capacity to get usable data from the study and to continue to justify their referral status with the judicial system was a t risk. Graduate students pursuit of funding, publications, and theses were at risk. Undergraduates' pursuit of admission to the graduate program and the building of collegial relationships to that end were at risk. The "patients" however, were in the somewhat enviable position, referenced in Marxist thought in that they "had nothing to lose but their chains."

During this stage of my observation, there began to be a rebellion against the rigidity of the program by selected members of the staff. This rebellion ironically resulted in the best week of interaction with the youth I had witnessed, but was not to have much effect on the programmatic imperative I have been relating. This was because the revolt was discussed in the vocabulary of the status quo and attributed to the flexibility and dynamism of the design rather than situational ingenuity on the part of the counselors.

"RISK ASSESSMENT"

In the meetings with the staff held before the sessions the staff continued to grapple with the question of what to do with the undergraduates. A dispute had arisen over the requirements that had been imposed upon them and whether they were reasonable given the students lack of experience and expertise. Of particular concern was their assignment to prepare an annotated bibliography of qualitative research on the treatment of juvenile delinquency. I found it interesting that this concern about preparation had not been raised as an issue in terms of the students' roles as counselors for very young children, roles I found a lot more risky than allowing them to fend for themselves in search of unfamiliar references. Raised anew was the question of whether the prospective introduction of more new people into the site and the effect that would have. It was agreed by the staff that their introduction should be delayed for an additional week to offer the families a "rest" from the penetration that had occurred earlier and which the staff felt may have induced some of the problems experienced within the sessions.

Dr. Wind indicated that he would be out of town for a conference on poverty stricken families and counseling related to their situation. As a consequence of his absence, it was agreed that the pre-session meeting would not be held the following week. This brought concerns from Marsha, who feared that some major development would occur during Wind's absence for which she would not be prepared. She insisted that he produce a contact number of some sort, just in case.

Discussion then turned to the undergraduates' work on the "things-to-do" guide for youth during the summer. The undergraduates first noted that the churches had been unhelpful and then gave Marsha, the material that had been gathered, mainly from library sources. They were particularly happy that they had been able to find a program that catered to girls, since the general body of literature had been oriented towards contact sports and boys. At this point I raised the issue of "risk assessment," and was pleased when Dr. Wind stated that he had finally received the documentation he had requested from Nixon concerning the matter and that I could copy them after the meeting. I greeted this information with a sense of relief since I had had up to this point, had considerable difficulty in procuring risk assessment material. I planned to review the material and then interview Nixon about any particulars that intrigued me or that seemed relevant to the program's definition of "risk." Such an interview became unnecessary when Nixon arrived with startling revelations.

It seemed likely to Dr. Wind that the transfer of the existing "risk assessment" facility to city hands would come sooner than later and that this necessitated a reevaluation of its role within the program. Marsha, on the other hand, thought that any facility movements would be more likely to occur in the fall. Nixon indicated that he was surprised at the rapidity of developments. Dr. Wind's pointed questioning of Nixon resulted in a kind of "organic interview" concerning the overall rationale of "risk assessment."

The first question was how much data had been gathered in association with "risk assessment." This revealed the fact that it was the risk assessment component, and not the therapeutic component of the data that was generating the quantitative material. Moreover, it revealed this component as essential to the progress of the program from a research standpoint. The answer was that some data had been collected, but not an inordinate amount. Follow-ups involved questions about how the "risk assessments" were going. Nixon responded that things were proceeding at a rather slow pace. The interaction between the staff and Nixon provided major insight into internal conflicts over definitions within the program staff corps. Nixon's frequent absences, like Dee's, were less a function of scheduling conflicts than disagreement about some of the basic suppositions of the program. He was genuinely detached and decidedly noncommittal when asked whether assessments should or would continue. Dr. Wind effectively began to reel in the discussion by stating unequivocally "I'd hate to lose all that good data [gathered from the assessments]."

Given this authoritarian line, the debate changed to where the assessments should be held. Nixon maintained that it was not worth fighting in court over the existing facility because suitable substitutes could be found. The two sites under primary consideration were the clinic and the courthouse, with the relative merits of each being considered. The courthouse offered the advantage of proximity for the participants but had the stigma of being attached to the legal realm. The clinic offered no such stigma, but involved greater distance and potential problems with parking. The issue was not firmly resolved, but I left feeling convinced that the clinic had the upper hand.

Next, discussion turned to staffing for the program. Nixon indicated that traditionally he had operated alone in the process, occasionally retaining an assistant to assist "clients" in filling out the forms. I noted that he had apparently encountered enough difficulty with the forms that he had been motivated to hire someone. How much, I wondered, did this "help" influence the results? He suggested, in response to a counter-suggestion by Dr. Wind, that the position be restricted to someone with clinical experience who could devote at least twelve hours per week to the effort. When asked why, he began to note many aspects of his experience. There was no binding authority upon the families to submit to the assessment and he had to engage in a process of "convincing" them that it would be in their best interest. He, like other staff members, was offended that families would enter the assessment setting with a desire to discuss the nature of the legal dispute involving their youth(s). That was not his concern. They were constantly complaining that they were not being "listened to." He stated that their reactions involved various levels of resistance and in some cases, anger. Many of the families would come with the expectation that he would be a counselor or advocate for their interests, a status he considered clearly beyond his responsibilities.

SANS TEXT

In the youth session, Dan had again departed, leaving Geraldine in charge. She began in the usual manner, with the text-based approach addressing questions about life at home. The situation became considerably more tense when [Q] responded to this line of inquiry by suggesting that she would "rather be dead right [then]." This was more an allusion to the youths' sense of boredom with the sessions, exacerbated by the program's character. Several youth corroborated the feeling. Nothing, except in the case of [L], suggested that there were suicidal tendencies on the part of group members. They were merely registering their discontent and it was out of frustration that these comments were made. Geraldine responded by emphasizing the extent to which youth was a phase that would be outgrown and that things were never as bad as they seemed. She focused, in her remarks, on the need to "enjoy" childhood experiences, since adult responsibilities would not be as romantic as the youth may have thought.

Geraldine wanted my intervention at this point. Eager to strike a more realistic tone about death, I offered a personal experience in which I had actually contemplated participating in acts that would likely have resulted in my own death. My point was that the reality of death is quite unlike the mere contemplation of a cessation of life's travails, and that there was a responsibility in living. This seemed to have a profound effect upon the tenor of group comments, away from the morbidity. In my mind, the psychological and physical safety of the youth could have been endangered by the consideration of suicide as a methodology for escaping from the program and from the social problems that generated it.

The discussion continued, listlessly. At the point of exasperation, Geraldine went into an approach distinctly different from that suggested by the text. It involved two techniques. One was to extend textual questions into realms that piqued youth responses. The second was to ask them explicitly to identify what it was that they wanted to talk about. Geraldine's role as a counselor changed from the moderator of a structured discussion to a participant in a democratic circle of conversation with little or no influence over the direction of the talk. Admitting the structure's material failure and liberating the youth brought forth a flood of interest and involvement. Beginning with the notion of parental restriction, the youth pointed out that they understood that such restrictions were in place to protect them from harm [in contrast to the discussion that followed in the larger group where a lack of knowledge about rules was posited as a basis for familial conflict]. They then discussed "Grand Slam," a city-county combined government facility that stages social gatherings for youth during the summer, as an example of a program that allows youth autonomy while providing rules against weapons and excessive interpersonal shows of affection, answering parental concern for safety. There was a general longing for more of these types of programs and more generally, within their lives, a balancing of autonomy and constraint different from the ones they were experiencing.

Geraldine then led us through the textual backdoor to the question of the role of peer pressure in affecting behavior and resistance to parental authority, renewing the debate over friends and their "acceptability" to parents. It also involved talk about the characteristics that make certain individuals good potential friends. The discussion began to lag again, punctuated by several youth saying things like "This is so stupid," "I'm tired of these [sessions]," and "Oh, Jesus!," (the latter comment courtesy of [L]). [Q], the youth who made the other two comments, emphasized her distaste for this by turning away from the general discussion, working on her toenails, and twirling her earrings.

In response, Geraldine again shifted gears away from the text and to interpersonal obligations. This subject had come up in the context of the discussion on friends and the youth seemed to have some interest. The debate turned on the issue of ethical conflict, those cases in which a friend or accompanying individual violates the law and what, if any obligation one has to stand by the individual in the event of social sanction. Consistent with my earlier hypothesis about the "honor" aspect of culturally subordinated groups, all of the youth maintained that one stands by his or her friends regardless of the consequences, each citing evidence of situations in which he or she received punishment for supporting others in illegal or "socially inappropriate" acts. These experiences were voiced as obligations and duties. Despite Geraldine's subtle suggestion that one should look out for his or her self as well as the friend(s) by refusing to participate in and discouraging such behavior, the youth maintained a collectivist mentality as well as the right to define those that were worthy of identification with them and at what level. The youth explained the difference between "friends" and "associates."

"Friends" seems to have the traditional connotation that most of us think of when we talk about friends. "Associates" on the other hand, seemed to denote those who were "friends" at some past time, but whose actions have been such as to cause estrangement in the relationship, either by parental approbation or personal choice. What was striking was the extent to which the obligations of one to "friends" and "associates" were the same, implying a kind of adherence to an implied code of honor and dual responsibility that can supersede even personal disagreements and transgressions and extend to one's whole socio-cultural group.

As the group was composed primarily of African-American women, it was interesting to note also that the discussion of same sex "friends" and "associates" and conflicts hinged on relationships with men. Emphasis was given to African men's seemingly insatiable appetite for infidelity and the "proper" response for dealing with it. The young African men in the room tended to withdraw from the discussion at this point, since they were "out-gunned." Geraldine even legitimated this ostracism by saying that her comments on the matters being discussed might "get her in trouble with Imani" even though she did not know I shared some of her critical sentiments. The program provided no African male role model commiserate with Geraldine that could take up their defense in this gender polarized discussion and as a result, they felt isolated. This was evidenced by the manner in which they talked to one another but did not introduce any of their discordant comments to the larger group. The men were assumed to have multiple girlfriends as a matter of course. African women's proper reaction to this presumed truth was to act as if this they didn't know until confronted by the other women. Likewise, African women were seen as victims of jealousy and a desire to exploit "gaps" in relationships for gain. Both images are of course derivative of the classic "whore" and "pimp" images that emanated from the historical use of the reproductive capability of African women as a marketable good and the breeding of African males as sires for slaves (Clarke et al. 1983; Davis 1981; Hooks 1981; King 1973). Geraldine emphasized that in an incident of infidelity involving the male, the male and not the female was at fault and should be solely punished. One young woman even went so far as to say that she had punched a male who had been unfaithful. I found it interesting again, that a counselor in a program for legally endangered first offenders did not directly counter this admittance of and assertion of the validity of such violence, because it was inflicted on a "deserving" male. Beyond this there was no programmatic requirement to challenge the divisive notions being set forth as the youth theoretically constructed definitions of their experience. Such requirements did exist when the behavior affected the Eurocentric social order, say in the form of shoplifting or drugs, but the program was decidedly silent when acts were manifested within one's own socio-cultural group.

The youth session went on for a considerably longer period than usual on the grounds that more beneficial discussion was taking place. [L] asked me specifically what time it was as a sign of her impatience. When she stated to those near her that it was "time to go," the discussion began to unravel and the fatigue of group and counselor began to show. The youth expressed discontent because they had learned when it was time to go to "snack" and the abrupt program change caught them off guard.

RATIONALE FOR DEVIANCE

The combined session was brief, this time focusing on "rules." Each parent and child was asked to prepare a list of household rules, as well as of the rewards and punishments associated with those rules to see if there was a degree of correspondence. The need to pass out pencils and paper merged with waning time resulting in the generation only lukewarm response to this request. The responses that were received suggested that there was common knowledge of the rules of the households in spite of the program's preliminary suppositions. The problem was enforcement, and Dee again reached into her own experience, offering negotiation and cooperation as the key to resolving the problems of noncompliance. For the third consecutive session, discord rumbled through the parents' crowd as the prospect of negotiating parents still did not sell. At this point, Geraldine and me began an enlightening conversation. I began by complimenting her on what I thought was a great improvisational performance in the youth group. She corroborated my observation that her alteration of the program was a response to the general disinterest in the topics presented in the text and greater interest in other things. She also agreed that there was a cultural aspect to the whole issue of negotiating with children. Her parents like mine, were disinclined to such interactive diplomacy on questions of juvenile responsibility.

MORE RATIONALIZING

Immediately after the sessions, there was the usual debriefing and the central topic was the suicide solution rhetoric on the part of the youth and whether that had any actual meaning. I raised the issue since no staff member seemed to identify this situation as a problem. They pointed out that in the case of [Q], no evidence indicated any friction between her and her mother, in fact she was depicted as the ideal responsible child. This observation was based on appearances in the sessions. Linda chimed in, however, with a slightly different view gathered from her discussions with the mother which suggested that [Q] was very dependent in their relationship and as such, might be experiencing a degree of insecurity. Rather than recommending counseling to grapple with this insecurity, the response by the senior staff members was to reintegrate this dissonant information back into the initial perspective. Any perceived suicide statements were diagnosed as intended to garner attention. As such, they were to be disregarded for any real implication of suicidal tendencies or of programmatic failure.

A similar reintegration took place in the case of [M], whose mother Marsha had spoken to and inquired about solutions to his propensity for violent responses to situations. This sentiment Marsha prefaced with some background suggesting that [M] had been brutalized as a child. This was countered by Geraldine in an analysis that I agreed with at the time, that [M] was very reserved and quiet or "cool" in the sessions, speaking when spoken to and being generally polite. This observation was then fit into the developing thesis by pointing out that rarely did the situation arise in the sessions for a violent response [discourse was voluntary]. As such, response ranges would be limited and no judgment could be made. The issue was dropped. The meeting then concluded.

ASSESSMENT AT RISK

I reviewed the "risk assessment" material before the next session. I received the youth form and a form for female parents, but not one for male parents. This suggests the persistence of certain familial structure assumptions on the part of the program. The forms themselves were singularly unimpressive given the web of secrecy which surrounded them. They essentially bore out the framework suggested in the program's documentary material with an emphasis on those variables that were supposed to suggest a propensity towards increasing levels of familial dysfunctionality. What was most interesting was the level of diction employed in the questions. Given the relatively low level of formal education of the participants, it seemed likely that whatever data may have been gathered using these forms were mere reflections of the individual hired to help respondents complete them rather than real measures of variables.

LESSONS LEARNED: POTENTIAL FOR SYNTHESIS

Clearly, the discussion recorded in this chapter benefited most from the abandonment within the youth session of the textual curriculum in favor of a more fluid, indeterminate focus group discussion. The unwillingness to do so in the large discussion continued to mean that contributions from the intuitive knowledge bases of the parents were excluded. Where the youth session failed is in the realm of the recognition of socio-cultural oppression and in the lack of any provision for culturally relevant solutions. The program's epistemology prevented success in both cases. If one takes the view that Africans are like all "Americans," one does not look for unique problems affecting them. Nor does one look for a unique cause that might be different from the cause of the same malady in non-African social groups.

The multicultural critique, in this case, would focus again on the issue of cognitive and cultural styles. Specifically, this examination would focus on cross-cultural communicative competencies on the part of the program staff.

Central to comprehending the youths' structures of meaning around the concepts of honor and respect necessitates consideration of the fact of and the manner in which they have internalized the images of themselves rendered by an oppressive dominant culture. This internalization however, is not a passive process. It is a dialectic that involves the re-articulation of dominant culture values as received into an approximation of the subordinated group's own.

Respect is held in the highest honor as a Eurocentric collective moral value. It is similarly a value within the cultural ethos of Africans. The contradiction involves the justification of the means by which respect is to be affected. In mainstream parlance, respect is earned specifically by equally culturally defined norms of legality and ethics. The African youth view traditional modes of soliciting respect as foreclosed for a number of reasons. Consequently, the cultural imperative for respect is reshaped to facilitate its acquisition by those means which are available. For example, respect from the larger society is not often forthcoming, so more important is respect in one's own collective. Such respect would be relevant outside of the context of a system of oppression, but in the latter case its relative importance is penultimate. Within the community, the modes of garnering respect are limited in terms of economics and the "American dream." Familiar social structures like the family and more specifically, personal relationships become repositories for leftover aspirations to honor and respect. A man begins to be judged by how well he controls his woman in a relationship, an idea antithetical to the African ideal of relationship. A woman is judged by her ability to elude that control. What's left is a series of relationships that reify general social stereotypes about the African family and about the socio-eco-political relationships between African men and women that function neither as mutual support structures nor as stores of cultural knowledge [as they did in the past]. What a multicultural perspective would realize is that the parallel in form between the words used to describe a culturally bound value within two or more groups may be a hindrance to the development of a healthy multicultural personality, since power makes one definition superior and evaluative of the other. As for the joint session, the continual effort to get African parents to assimilate the Eurocentric cultural ethos about "democracy" and such approaches to parenting shows a lack of respect for the need to incorporate the patient's perspective rather than the theoretician's.

An Africentric psychological perspective would repeat the admonition about the parents while focusing in on the essential phenomenological experiential context for understanding African experience. Both the parents and the youths' knowledge claims are advanced through a careful interpretation of historical knowledge about what works within the particular social context in which they live. What the staff is asking, by virtue of the curriculum is for Africans to step outside of their "realities" and play according to rules that would be logical and applicable in the new locale. Africentric psychologists would see such an undertaking as useless from the therapeutic sense, since the essential knowledge base from which to make a diagnosis and make prescriptions has been eliminated as a source of data.

Within the Africa-centered psychological context, any adequate evaluation of the youth's comments on gender relationships within the African-American community would have to consider how these young women's perspectives on themselves, on African men, and upon their relationship to the latter men is predicated upon Eurocentric cultural dominance. Such an analysis would explain their experiences in light of such an ideological system. As counselors, they would begin "treatment" with the notion that, in an African-centered evaluation of infidelity, both the man and women are at fault. Moreover, the problems extend to their familial units and to their youth socialization process.

Chapter Six

"De-Brief" and "Hack"

The term "hacker" has two distinct meanings contingent upon the view that one has concerning the activity in which such people operate. To the sympathetic ear, the hacker is the organic democracy advocate of the technological age. The "hacker ethic" is to demand complete access to computers and to anything which might shed light on the manner in which the world works (Levy, 1984). In a critical view, such individuals are engaging in sabotage, casually breaking into others' computer systems in order to alter or thieve the information therein.

To the hacker, the non-hacker's "machine" is an abstract system running according to mathematical laws. The hacker is merely an inhabitant of the abstract domain. His or her ethic is a form of subversion that refuses to submit to corporate control.

It is also possible to "hack" into other systems of control including psychological and ideological control. In this sense, hacking is the repeatedly juxtaposition of empirical realities and derivative narratives against a set of dominating ideological presuppositions. It is, in the colloquial sense, "speaking truth to power." Throughout the psychotherapeutic interaction in the program, the clients and certain staff members were speaking uncomfortable and disconcerting truths. While the validity of most of the narratives remained unscathed, there had developed a very elaborate system of internal rationalization and nullification. This system sustained the integrity and legitimacy of the program. Of particular destructive capacity are those truths that strike at the heart of the instrumental rationality of the system. In this case, the stated intention of the program was to rebuild these family structures into a state of psychological normalcy and thereby avoid recidivism. The arguments that the families in question were in fact, normal already is therefore extremely menacing.

73

If we characterize "head games" as an effort at psychological colonization, then "hacking" can be understood to be a method of brining about a kind of voluntary collective "de-briefing" in which the oppressive grip of the psycho-therapeutic suppositions are broken and turned in on themselves.

THE EFFECT OF COMPETING
SOCIO-CULTURAL NARRATIVES

Likewise, the emergent and competing socio-cultural narratives in the program emanating from clients and staff alike, unwittingly, ends up "hacking" into the psychological programming at the heart of the therapeutic effort. More often than not, the program failed to convince the youth or their parents of the validity of its arguments. Sometimes the parents and youth "figured out" that a social engineering project was in progress and declined to behave in ways conducive to the continuation of the programmatic agenda. Sometimes they posited knowledge claims that sent the staff into theoretical retreat. Finally, they periodically presented information imbedded within these claims that forced the staff to rationalize the discrepancies between occurrences and their epistemological and ontological expectations.

PREPPING FOR "CLOSURE?"

As I went to the final session, I found myself more relaxed and calm, having developed a degree of familiarity with the site and having developed rapport with the personnel of the program. I contemplated how I would negotiate my departure. I decided that I had to give back something to the youth. I decided to make myself available to the youth, via an address, to assist them in their academic or vocational aspirations.

I arrived early enough to run into [L], her mother and her siblings and one other parent en route to the meeting room. The chairs had already been set up. I then ran into Brooke. After some introductory chatter about our mutual feelings that evening, she mentioned that she detected a great deal of anxiety and tension in the responses she had received upon greeting the program staff. This information was beneficial, as I too sensed that something was dreadfully wrong. Arriving at the moment Brooke imparted this information were Kirk and Dee and I talked to them about their general state of health. Also present was an graduate student who had been involved in the process of quantitative data entry for the program and wanted to observe the program in actual operation.

When we arrived in the general assembly room, I understood better what the staff had addressed repeatedly over the preceding weeks, the possibly of overcrowding. There was that one graduate student as well as a large number of siblings, "friends," and "associates" of the youth in the program making the group look "surrounded." One of the mothers remarked, "I've never been around so many white folk in my life." That comment struck me, because it was what had crept into my mind at precisely that same moment. Standing directly above her were the three Euro-American female undergraduates, the two Euro-American counselors, and the "guest."

KILL THE MODERATOR!

In the youth session, I watched as Dan [Geraldine was absent] steered the group back to the rigid, textual and visual format outlined in the manual. The level of participation was consequentially minimal. This was accompanied by a rather heavy-handed rhetorical style that probably did as much to intimidate all concerned as to discourage interaction. Things got off to the wrong start when he inquired as to [Q's] well-being. She responded that she was "ok." He responded," You don't sound convincing." I wondered whether her statements about her feelings were to be subjected to some kind of validity test, with him being the arbiter. The subject for the session was anger, and this was perhaps most fitting in the sense that [L] entered the session angrily. Dan proved ineffective at handling the situation. He began by likening anger to pain, suggesting that it was an emotive and physical response designed to provide us with protection from harm. This is clearly a Eurocentric framework, philosophically separating the "emotive" realm from the "pragmatic."

Bologh criticizes Max Weber's work on religion, in which he draws an irrevocable dichotomy between "rational" and "ecstatic" religions and draws out the implications of each of these for social action. In his view, "emotive" refers to the appeal to the senses as a means for inculcating a particular ethical maxim within an individual or reinforcing preexisting ethical predilections. "Pragmatic" conversely deals with the formulation of "logical" (in the Platonic sense), usually sequential, arguments that appeal to individuals' intellects as a source of legitimacy. While Bologh focuses on the implications for constructions of sex and gender, I would point out that such a view is also problematic within an Africentric socio-psychological methodology because therein, opposites are same in nature, different in kind. It is therefore quite rational to be emotive, and rational responses presumably would involve emotion.

Dan next asked the youth to complete the phrase "When I am angry I usually ----." The student responses came in two categories: (a) withdrawal from the conflict situation and (b) fighting. The critical element in determining which of these two options was to be chosen in any given situation was the subjectively perceived power of the opposing party or force. Dan responded by saying that he usually "acts like he isn't angry and goes about his business." Such internalization would be more likely to induce psychological disease than security. The next phrase was "One person who made me angry was ----." Among the accounts was the situation in which [B] said a friend had wounded him in the head with a BB gun. Dan's reaction to this was uproarious laughter, a response that ultimately resulted in laughter on the part of the other youth, despite the fact that [B] spoke of the experience with great trepidation. The laughter, keynoted by Dan, rose to a fever pitch when [B] stated that he had responded to this injury by trying to inflict a similar injury on his fleeing playmate. It was unclear whether he ever caught the friend and "paid him back."

The fact that Dan, the Euro-American counselor, found such unprovoked violence against [B] by another African male and the confrontation that ensued as funny, made me angry for the second time in as many sessions with him, and I began to suspect that his personal opinion of African males was low.

Dan even went as far as to accuse one youth of lying when he stated that he did not get mad. In the course of this discussion, [L] entered, late, and asked whether Geraldine would be coming. Dan responded that Geraldine had called Dee and that she had business to attend to in another southern city, different from the first, and that she might not be able to attend. [L] reacted with a clear disdain for this turn of events and turned away from Dan, not participating in the proceedings at all.

Dan next turned to the video images for the week, essentially a lot of the same material the youth had seen in preceding weeks. I noticed that there was an assumption that the three films selected [Boyz N' Tha Hood, Juice, and Do The Right Thing] had been seen by all of the youth, and that these were sufficient to represent African culture. This assumption was incorrect. Moreover, I became aware that Dan had not seen enough of the films to understand their contextual meaning, and he presented several scenes incorrectly. Two of the examples of "anger" he chose were actually examples of remorse and inquisitiveness, features easily discerned by those who had both seen the films in their entirety and who were knowledgeable about African socio-culture.

And just when I thought things could get no worse, they did. He introduced a trailer from "Do The Right Thing" in which there were quotes from Reverend Doctor Martin Luther King Jr. and Minister El Hajj Malik el-Shabazz.

The first comment was too unclear to be dealt with, so Dan moved straight to the second. He interpreted Malcolm's comments as advocating violence and asked subjects what they thought. The problem was that the statements, like the clips they followed, were completely de-contextualized. Any use of force by African-Americans is considered violence. As a result, Malcolm's advocacy of self-defense for Africans is identified as the advocacy of violence. In the comments, Malcolm turns the tables on his detractors by embracing the very concept with which they sought to entrap him. He states implicitly that, if any use of force is violence, then violence must be legitimized in cases of self-defense. A more congenial socio-culture, allowing for the right of self-determination and self-defense, would not have forced Malcolm to this conclusion, as it would have made a clear demarcation between self-defense and violence. This was a complex rhetorical device frequently employed by Malcolm, but one that whites interpreted as placing him in direct opposition in strategy to Dr. King. Throughout the evolution of the civil rights movement, Reverend Doctor King was engaged in a complex "cat and mouse" game with the relevant local authorities, seeking to provoke violence while simultaneously containing it and using it to de-legitimate the pro-segregationist position. Dan clearly has little understanding of this African communicative tradition, and thus is left with only a literal interpretation to give to the youth who are forced to choose between two African leaders. The use of physical force is proscribed, even when the vast majority of the Africans in the program come from backgrounds in which the establishment of "honor" is paramount to social survival.

The poor fit between the ideology of the program and of the youth was perhaps best exemplified by [Q's] reaction, which involved hurling her jewelry across the room. To top it all off, we saw two more trailers pointing out that one of twenty-one African males is killed, the majority of those deaths coming at the hand of other African males. Dan diagnosed this as simply a case of "anger out of control." Such reductionism I found astounding in its fallacy, and also dangerous. [Lt] in fact, voiced my fears when she implied that the men "had to be doing something to [deserve] that situation." Dan lamely responded that the issue of desert was not discussed in the trailer, but offered no counter-thesis, leaving hers as the final conclusion. At the end of the meeting, [L] did not move, and was later found to be crying. Dan and Dee rushed to intervene.

Ironically, during this same session, [Q] had complimented me on the African animal necklace I was wearing and asked where I had bought it. I told her and offered to procure her one if she would like. In the snack pause her mother added the caveat "if she's good [implying that she would employ it as some sort of "bargaining chip"]. I noted here that the "ideologizing" was beginning to have some effect. At the end of the abbreviated combined session, true to my word, I gave [Q] my address and asked her to remind me about the necklace. She seemed genuinely happy, and this made for a small bright spot in a sea of pain, that I was able to give something back and in this case something out of African socio-culture back to a sister whose insight had paved the way for many of the interesting data items herein.

IMPLOSION

The usual snack break ensued, but about halfway into it, one could tell the program was disintegrating. Many of the youth had gone outside and were wandering with limited supervision. Many of the parents had likewise wandered very far away or had left entirely. Dee announced, after a fifteen minute delay, that we were to begin in five minutes. She also asked [L's] mother to accompany her upstairs to the youth session room. After twenty more minutes, Dee had not returned and Marsha passed me, looking somewhat flustered. I said, "what's going on?" Before she could answer, Dee had returned. Strangely, she was perplexed as to why everyone was leaving. Marsha pressed her to conclude the session and all of the remaining parents and youth were hurriedly rounded up into a group. Dee apologized for her "rude" absence, but then paradoxically reversed the tone by stating that the parents were being rewarded for their consistent attendance by this early departure. She announced that she would distribute worksheets on the lesson that was supposed to have been discussed, rewards and punishments, but stated explicitly that the parents had the right to ignore them. She then insisted upon a rather disorganized group hug, at which I announced my departure as well as my intent to leave a contact number with the counselors should anyone wish to reach me. I thanked the participants for letting me be a part of their "family." Dee then hurried upstairs to where the situation with [L], I later found out, was reaching catastrophic proportions.

What I thought was most striking about this breakdown was the fact that it was a direct consequence of the organization of the system rather than any error on the part of staff members. In their efforts to effect maximum penetration of the families in terms of counseling, they had assigned many of the participants to the formal therapy program. As a result, the counselors had dual roles. In practice, they desired to keep these two roles separate, with the program occurring at its time, and the counseling being otherwise scheduled. [L's] situation necessitated the presence of Dee and Dan, her case handlers, and it was the former who was supposed to lead the group session. There seemed to be no one prepared to "take her place" despite the availability of the text, nor did anyone except Marsha [out of exasperation] move to do something about the situation of the parents and youth who were waiting for the session to start.

REQUIEM FOR MY SISTER

We moved upstairs for the debriefing session at which I raised the concerns I had concerning the de-contextualization of the visual images and the mis-interpretation of the data on African males. Marsha responded that I needed to take this matter up with Dan personally, with a tone that signaled to me that it was time to leave the scene. Since my departure was anticipated by the staff, I was gradually becoming seen as an "outsider" again and my "pass" was about to be revoked. I was no longer a consultant and wanted critic, but a type of "holdover" whose time had come and gone. She also pointed out that the film usage was not mandatory. The program text itself did list explicit instructions concerning the use of videos. Marsha stated that she used them only for generating discussion and that she "didn't like them."

Periodically, we were interrupted by [L's] family members and siblings. Most disturbing was the fact that [L] had requested Brooke's phone number [hoping to use Brooke as a bulwark against Dan, who she really didn't like]. Marsha responded by instructing the undergraduate [L] asked to [falsely] tell [L] that the program didn't have Brooke's number and that all of [L's] com-munication would have to be directed to Dan. This constituted an organiza-tional "closing of the ranks" around [L] and it had the effect I anticipated. [L] ran out of the building crying and at the time I left, had not yet been found. It amazed me that they did not allow [L] to make contact with Brooke, since she seemed willing to talk and they didn't quite know what was wrong with her. Moreover, to offer her her nemesis Dan as the only hope was, in her estimation, to offer nothing.

I left the site feeling a much greater sense of sadness. Given more time, [L] would have confided in me and I might have been able to save my sister from the Eurocentric behavioral models that she so desperately seemed to be resisting with her last strength and that the staff was so diligently imposing in analyzing her behavior. I will forever remember her pleasant greeting to me when she and her family arrived [no small honor, since she did not verbalize with those she did not trust and consider "ok"]. Behind those eyes, I didn't see a "dysfunctional" human being, but a scared, intimidated, young African woman, surrounded by an institutional structure that her socio-culture had had no part in creating and that was unwilling or incapable of giving her the vital sense of self-affirmation she needed to survive. Her "schizophrenia" was at best an embodiment of that curious African state of "being" but yet not being allowed to "become." As a self-defense mechanism she was withdrawing into herself and resisting all contact with the hostile "outside," except for that with a few intimates who pierced her "walls." Those walls are the walls of all Africans reified and extended. Euro-Americans fail to understand that the "dysfunctionality" their psychological theories repeatedly identify in the African community is the result of the historical application of similarly culturally bound theories and that the ideology that underpins them was forcibly imposed. Marsha said in our final meeting of [L] "what we've got here is a girl with a lot of serious problems." Perhaps the greatest problem [L] has is maintaining the fortitude to resist, without acting on her threats of suicide or tolerating any sexual abuse that may exist, those who would label her very manifestation of being as "dysfunctional," her family "deviant," and her people ultimately, inferior.

FINAL DISSOLUTION AND THEORETICAL INSIGHTS

As for the demise of this session, the multicultural perspective would find programmatic a lot of the discussion around socio-cultural images, in this case of Africans. All of these images have to be evaluated in terms of authenticity [that is to say are they socio-culturally bound or re-articulations of the dominant paradigms] and in terms of equality [there are no images inherently superior to the others]. The latter principle is fundamental for a therapist's acceptance of the multiplicity of different socio-cultures. If he or she does not adhere to the principle of equality, hierarchy and oppressive psychological analysis is the consequence. The act of evaluating cultural forms and manifestations without evaluating them as such and within the context of the meanings of the relevant social community is to misuse these. Juxtaposing Eurocentric cultural interpretations of African leaders [a process necessarily resulting in the placement of these in opposition], and pushing one image over another is cultural manipulation and control not psychological liberation and therapy.

An Africentric psychological perspective would argue similarly that there was insufficient socio-cultural grounding for the materials presented in the youth session and in the handling of the delicate situation involving the emotional and physical stability of the young African woman. As for the adult session, notes would be made of how easy it was for the staff to "give up" on the viability of the combined session. The ethos of the parents is to "keep on keepin' on" and many were genuinely offended when it appeared that they would be left waiting longer. Disrespect was therefore invoked and led to hard feelings which made it impossible to proceed with any degree of productivity.

From an African-centered perspective, the dichotomy employed by Dan in the youth session to explain the proper perspective on the films missed the constant dialectic between the "ecstatic" and "rational" aspects of the collective presentation of self among African-Americans and the interplay between these aspects that give the socio-culture its unique appearance and dynamic political character. In the African-American point of view, the "emotive" is not irrational. In fact, rationality demands an emotive response. As such, it is quite "irrational" to try and teach Africans to externalize their emotions in the Eurocentric sense.

Chapter Seven

Taking the Helmet Off

The "first offender" program might be best analyzed the framework proposed by Dorothy Smith (1993) on text-oriented discourse. In her article, "The Standard North American Family," she discussed the ways in which her use of Eurocentric analytical schemes and their associated "T-discourses" resulted in unintended replication of the ideological precepts she sought to critique. She argued that T-discourse was "a system of virtual relations coordinating, ordering, hooking up, the activities of individuals in multiple historical sites." Going beyond Foucault's conception of discourse as a conversation mediated by texts, she included how actual people took them up, the practices and courses of actions ordered by them, how they coordinated the activities of one with those of one another or others and emphasized that entry into such discourses could be in ordinary and "unthinking" ways and proposed that there are "ideological codes" that order and organize texts across discursive sites. Smith defined "ideological code" as a schema that "replicated its organization in multiple and various sites . . . a constant generator of procedures for selecting syntax, categories, and vocabulary in the writing of texts and the production or talk and for interpreting sentences. The standard North American family [hereafter SNAF] was conceived of as just such an ideological code.

This ideal form conceptualized a family as being constituted by "a legally married couple sharing a household. The adult male is in paid employment; his earnings provide the economic basis of the family household. The adult female may also earn income, but her primary responsibility is to the care of husband, household, and children." Even when such a form is not "prevailing" in the social milieu under investigation, it constituted the "basic unit from which more complex familial forms are compounded." This point was corroborated in a study by her research partner Alison Griffith (1984) which showed how the dysfunctionality suggested by a family unit which did not correspond to SNAF, provided for teachers' procedures for reading back from what could be observed in the classroom to the "defective" family. Such an analytical approach constituted a documentary method of interpretation that resulted in an inescapable tautology (Mannheim 1971). Observations were interpreted in light of ideology and ideology selected what constituted data for the observation. The school-mother-T discourse laid the primary responsibility for the child's school achievement and success as an adult upon the family, and particularly upon the mother.

A similar "discourse of dysfunctionality" exists within the "first offenders" program, with the discourse between the staff and professionals in the psychological community supplemented with one between them and the participants. This later discourse is fundamentally different than the one Smith describes in that the power relationships between the conversants is no longer equal (e.g. two academicians within a discipline) but rather unequal and pejorative in favor of one of the parties. It is also intercultural in that the discourse of the participants is normed in an entirely different cultural tradition than that of the majority of the subjects. When intercultural communication is extended over vast power differentials, discourse functions as part and parcel of an oppressive ideological system.

The work of Molefi Asante (1983) is particularly instructive on these points. Discussion of intercultural communication, in his formulation, is the examination of the power relationships that underpin such conversation. Misunderstandings can be interpreted as consequences of power imbalances. Mature and effective intercultural communication can only occur with changes in relative power differentials, affected in turn, by transformation of the material conditions of the people. Failure to convert the ideology generating the codes leaves the oppressed subject to the oppressors' standards of "right," "logical," and "reasonable," with the limits being drawn by those who wield preponderant economic, political, and cultural power.

Clearly, the power of identifying and thereby defining the "client" families lay in the hands of Nixon and his associates. Via risk assessment interviews and measurement devices, they were in position to construct a "risk profile" which, in turn, determined the level of penetration into the family by social intervention systems and established the legitimacy of the coercion involved in compelling participants to attend and complete the program "satisfactorily." To wit, the comments by Dee that the families would not have been there if they did not deserve it and by Geraldine that school problems might have been related to one's designation as a "problem child." Both comments emphasized the notion that the youth in the program, as well as the families from whence they come, were viewed as "dysfunctional" relative to some normative standard. This was even more evident in the risk assessment materials and methodology which replicated the kind of ideology selecting objects-objects suggesting ideology tautology that is characteristic of the documentary method of interpretation (Griffith 1984; Mannheim 1971; Smith 1993).

After a family was identified and placed in the program, the power of definition was transferred to the graduate staff [with the assistance of the undergraduates]. The program itself was organized in such a manner as to emphasize symbolically and literally the need for the family to assimilate to Eurocentric core culture and to values like individualism [which necessitated the use of "I" messages], the "rule" of law and order [which explained the emphasis on common knowledge of rules and responsibilities in the households], the protestant work ethic [which prioritized the need for youth to be "out of the house" and never idle as an antidote to criminality], and "liberal" democracy [which necessitated negotiation with youth]. Any occurrence in the sessions which was not specifically along the lines of the scripted program, which was assumed to be the appropriate way "back" to social responsibility, was handled rhetorically and programmatically in one of two ways. Either the individual or family involved would be identified as deviant in other ways [like the case in which the angry mother is suspected of drug abuse when she actually has a toothache or when Dan commits a battery against [M] to try to wake him up from sleep and "not paying attention] or [should external social forces intervene like the school system or the judicial system] the response that little can be done was given and the matter retired. This resulted in a situation where all actions were carefully reprocessed into the system and little internal constructive criticism of epistemology could be sustained. Either the program helped, the family was deemed as refusing to allow it to help, or external forces had intervened in ways beyond its concern. The option of program failure was ontologically prohibited.

The final stage, at graduation, was the stage at which the data were compiled and the process of definition passed into the hands, primarily, of the principal investigators, who situated it in a psychological literature discourse that was also normed upon the Eurocentric standard. And this standard prioritized quantitative or quantitatively-structured qualitative data meaning that interviews, ethnographies, textual analyses, and other methodological forms were not a part of the primary research tools of the researchers. Since the intercultural miscommunication existed and replicated power relations at the level of recipients apprehension of the program, staffers' transmission of the program and interpretation of the text, as well as the textual construction itself, precluded the effective consideration data that could have provided an insight into the manner in which the psychotherapeutic mission was being confounded and the operation of the system thwarted.

Even the proper identification by the program of the material conditions structuring power relations between Euro-Americans and Africans would not have changed the discourse. The program was manifestly unwilling or incapable of intervening in other social structures that constituted the referral components of social experience for the participants. I believe this was due to the fact that the successful transformation of the social conditions construct- ing the dysfunctionality [say improving the school relationship and thus alle- viating truancy patterns] presented a problem for the rationale of the program itself. If the families truly had the power to correct their problems and had the tools to make such solutions materialize, what then was the ultimate pur- pose of the program? Part of the approach of the program epistemologically replicated, through inaction, the circumstances which generated dysfunction- ality thus continuing the rationale for more programmatic components, more funding, and so on. This logic took on a life of its own as these expansions required their use as well as a definitional structure placed upon potential "clients" that justified them.

This encapsulates an argument I made in an article on revolutionary service versus community service (1993). Community service programs, for the most part, function with an eye towards maintaining a foothold in the communities that they serve, in a sense, to legitimate their own role. This is very self-re- garding, and its results in the creation of a proverbial service or "vanguard" elite that hoards the organizational training and resources over the heads of the "masses." The problem with this model, in addition to the fact that it is undemocratic, is the fact that it can never truly lead to liberation, for the rel- evant recipient population remains perpetually subject to the tools of libera- tion rather than users of them.

Community service projects engage in outreach rather than "inreach." This is due to the fact that the "vanguard" by virtue of its monopoly of the tools of liberation begins to regard itself as elite and begins to distinguish between itself and the population it is attempting to liberate. The best case scenario for the community service program worker is that he or she be able to perpetually institutionalize a response to the need(s) of the population being served. Even if systemic change renders this desire meaningless, the community servant takes pride in the act of service. As such, the enthusiasm of the community servants is cyclical and their actions tend to lack unity of purpose. There is no dominant goal that integrates them.

In the case of the "first offender" program, the tool of liberation is the knowledge and belief that the families are capable of solving their own prob- lems, a point codified in the textual documentation and research publications of the principals. The psychological staff assumes the role of the "vanguard" as it seeks to "show the dysfunctional families how they have the power to become functional." Needless to say, this process is not liberating, but results in the need for the family to become functional by adherence to the instruction of the "vanguard." This condition persists despite the oral assertion that the program "bubbles up" from the participants' socio-cultural contexts. Clearly, the staff reserves the right to consider itself "objective" and "above" the people being served, even to the point of positing definitions of situations for them or labeling families and their behaviors. The result is that the staff takes great personal pride in the role of surrogate family for the participants despite the high rate of recidivism, the chaos of sessions, and the general collapse of the programmatic structure.

In order to combat this psychotherapeutic "virtual reality," the program has to take into consideration of insights gained from the more useful cross-cultural psychological paradigms that are being developed, three of which we have examined.

References

Akbar, Na'im. 1977. Natural Psychology and Human Transformation. Chi.: World Community of Islam.

Akbar, Naim. 1984. Africentric Social Sciences for Human Liberation. in Journal of Black Studies, Vol. 14. No. 4. pp. 395–414. Beverly Hills, Ca.: Sage Publications, Inc.

Allen, W. R. 1978. The search for applicable theories of black family life. in Journal of Marriage and the Family. 40(1), 117–129.

Amini, J.M. 1972. An African Frame of Reference. Chi.: Institute for Positive Education.

Anderson, Elijah. 1990 Streetwise: Race, Class, and Change in an Urban Community. Chicago: University of Chicago Press.

Andersen, T. 1987. The reflecting team: dialogue and metadialogue in clinical work. in Family Process. Vol. 4. No. 26. pp. 415–428. New York: Nathan W. Ackerman Family Institute.

Anderson, H. and Goolishan, H.A. 1988. Human systems as linguistic systems: Preliminary and evolving ideas about the implications for clinical theory. in Family Process. Vol. 4. No. 27. pp. 371–394.

Ani, Marimba. 1994. Yurugu: An African-Centered Critique of European Thought and Behavior. Trenton, N.J.: Africa World Press.

Armstrong, Robert. 1975. Wellspring: On the Myth and Source of Culture. Berkeley: University of California Press. p. 115.

Aschenbrenner, J. 1975. Lifelines: Black families in Chicago. New York: Holt, Rinehart, and Winston.

Asante, Molefi. 1983. The ideological significance of afrocentricity in intercultural communication. in Journal of Black Studies. Vol. 14, No. 1, Sept. pp.3–19. Beverly Hills, California: Sage Publications, Incorporated.

Baldwin, James. 1963. The Fire Next Time. N.Y.: Dial Press.

Baldwin, J.A. 1976. Black psychology and black personality: some issues for consideration. in Black Books Bulletin. 4(3), 6–11, 65.

Ball, S.J. 1981. Beachside Comprehensive. London: Cambridge University Press.

Barbera-Stein, L. 1979. Access negotiations: comments on the sociology of the sociologist's knowledge. Paper presented at the 74th Annual Meeting of the American Sociological Association, August 1979, Boston.

Barthes, Roland. 1972. Mythologies. New York: Hill and Wang.

Becker, H.S. and Geer, B. 1960. Participant observation: the analysis of qualitative field data. in R. N. Adams and J. J. Preiss (eds.) Human Organization Research: Field Relations and Techniques. Homewood, Ill.: Dorsey Press.

Benney, Mark and Everett C. Hughes. 1956. Of sociology and the interview. in American Journal of Sociology. Vol. 62. pp. 137–142. Chicago: University of Chicago Press.

Bigus, O.E. 1972. The milkman and his customer: a cultivated relationship. in Urban Life and Culture. Vol. 1. pp. 131–65.

Block, Carolyn. Black Americans and the cross cultural counseling and psychotherapy experience. in A.J. Marsella and P.Pederson, eds. Cross Cultural Counseling and Psychotherapy: Foundations, Evolutions, and Cultural Considerations. Elmsford, N.Y.: Pergamon Press.

Blumer, Herbert. 1969. Symbolic Interactionism. Englewood Cliffs, N.J.: Prentice-Hall.

Bologh, Roslyn Wallach. 1990. Love or Greatness. Boston.: Unwin Hayman.

Borges, Jorge Luis. 1970. The library of Babel. in Labyrinths. Penguin: London. p. 81.

Briggs. 1983. Questions for the ethnographer: a critical examination of the role of the interview in fieldwork. in Semiotica. Vol. 46. pp. 233–261. Hague: Mouton.

———. 1984. Learning how to ask: native metacommunicative competence and the incompetence of fieldwork. in Language and Society. Vol. 13. pp. 1–28.

Buck, M. 1977. Peer counseling from a black perspective. in The Journal of Black Psychology. 4(1), 15–28.

Bulhan, H.A. 1985. Frantz Fanon and the psychology of oppression. Plenum Publishing: N.Y.

Burton, L.M. 1991. Caring for children in The American Enterprise. May/June, pp.34–37. Washington, D.C.: American Enterprise Institute.

Burlew, A. Kathleen Hoard, Banks, W. Curtis, McAdoo, Harriette Pipes, and Azibo, Daudi Ajani ya. 1992. African American Psychology: Theory, Research, and Practice. Newbury Park: Sage.

Burlew, A. Kathleen Hoard, Smith, Willam David, Mosely, Myrtis Hall, and Whitney, W. Monty. 1979. Reflections on Black Psychology. University Press of America: Washington, D.C.

Carey, James T. 1972. Problems of access and risk in observing drug scenes. in Jack D. Douglas. ed. Observations of Deviance. pp. 314–26. New York: Random House.

Cicourel, A. V. 1967. Fertility, family planning, and the social organization of family life: some methodological issues. in Journal of Social Issues. Vol. 23. No. 4. pp. 57–81. New York: Society for the Psychological Study of Social Issues.

————. 1982. Interviews, surveys, and the problem of ecological validity. in American Sociologist. Vol. 17. pp. 11–20. Washington, D.C.: American Sociological Association.

Clarke, Cheryl, Gomez, Jewell J, Hammonds, Evelyn, Johnson, Bonnie, and Powell, Linda. 1983. Conversations and Questions: Black Women on Black Women Writers. in Conditions:Nine. Vol. 3, No. 3, 88–137. Brooklyn, New York: Conditions.

Clark, R.M. 1983 Family Life and School Achievement: Why Poor Black Children Succeed or Fail. Chicago: University of Chicago Press.

Collins, M. 1954. Cortez and Montezuma. Avon Books: N.Y.

Comaz-Diaz, L. and Griffith, E.E. (Eds.) 1982. Clinical Guidelines in Cross-cultural Mental Health. Wiley: N.Y.

Crevecoeur, J. H. St. J. 1904. Letters from an American farmer. Fox Duffield and Co.: N.Y.

Cubberly, E.P. 1909. Changing conceptions of education. Houghton Mifflin: Boston.

Davis, Angela Y. 1981. Women, Race, and Class. New York: Random House.

de Shazer, S. 1985. Keys to solution in brief therapy. New York: Norton.

————. 1988. Clues: Investigating solutions in brief therapy. New York: Brunner/Mazel.

Dean, J. P. and Whyte, W. F. 1958. How do you know if the informant is telling the truth? in Human Organization. Vol. 17. pp. 34–8.

Doherty, William J. and Macaran A. Baird. Family Therapy and Family Medicine Toward the Primary Care of Families. New York: Guilford Press.

Douglas, Jack. 1927. Observing deviance. in Jack D. Douglas ed. Research on Deviance. pp. 3–34. New York: Random House.

————. 1976. Investigative Social Research. Beverly Hills, Calif.: Sage.

Douglas, Jack D., and John M. Johnson, eds. 1977. Existential Sociology. New York: Cambridge University Press.

Everhart, R. B. 1977. Between stranger and friend: some consequences of "long-term" fieldwork in schools. in American Educational Research Journal. Vol. 14 (1), pp. 1–15.

Frake, 1964. Notes on queries in ethnography. in Transcultural Studies in Cognition. in American Anthropologist special edition. A.K. Romney and R.G. D'Andrade eds. Vol. 66. No. 3. Pt. 2. pp. 132–145. Washington, D.C.: American Anthropological Association.

————. 1977. Plying frames can be dangerous: some reflections on methodology in cognitive anthropology. in Quarterly Newsletter of the Institute for Comparative Human Development. Vol. 1. No. 3. pp. 1–7.

Freud, S. 1925 [1961]. Some psychological consequences of the anatomical distinction between the sexes. in J. Strachey (ed. and trans.) The standard edition of the complete psychological works of Sigmund Freud. Vol. 19. Hogarth Press: London.

Fuller, Neely Jr. 1969. The United Independent Compensatory Code/System/Concept: a textbook/workbook for thought, speech and/or action for victims of racism (white supremacy). Copyrighted, Library of Congress.

Gibson, William. 1986. Neuromancer. London: Grafton.

Glaser, B. and Strauss, A. 1967. The Discovery of Grounded Theory. Chicago, Ill: Aldine.

Glasgow, D.G. 1980. The Black Underclass: Poverty, Employment, and the Entrapment of Ghetto Youth. San Francisco: Jossey-Bass.

Goffman, Erving. 1963. Stigma. Englewood Cliffs, N.J.: Prentice-Hall.

———. 1972. Interaction Ritual. Harmondsworth: Penguin.

Goode, Erica. 2000. How culture molds habits of thought in New York Times August 8th.

Grier, William, and Cobbs, Price. Black Rage. N.Y.: Basic Books.

Griffith, A. 1984. Ideology, Education, and Single-Parent Families: The Normative Ordering of Families Through Schooling. Unpublished doctoral dissertation, University of Toronto.

Guthrie, R.V. 1976. Even the Rat was White. Harper and Row: N.Y.

Gutman, Herbert. 1976. The Black Family in Slavery and Freedom, 1750-1925. New York: Random House.

Hall, E.T. 1977. Beyond Culture. Garden City, N.Y: Anchor.

Hammersley. M. 1980. A peculiar world? teaching and learning in an inner city school. Ph.D. thesis. University of Manchester.

———. 1983c. The researcher exposed: a natural history. in Robert G. Burgess (ed.) The Research Process in Educational Settings. Lewes: Falmer.

Hannerz, U. 1969. Soulside: Inquiries into Ghetto Culture and Community. New York: Columbia University Press.

Hargreaves, D.H. 1967. Social Relations in a Secondary School. London: Routledge and Kegan Paul.

Havelock, Eric. 1967. Preface to Plato. New York: Grosset and Dunlap. p. 182, 200.

Hitchcock, G. 1983. Fieldwork as practical: reflections on fieldwork and the social organization of an urban, open-plan primary school. in M. Hammersley (ed.) The Ethnography of Schooling: Methodological Issues. Driffield: Nafferton.

Holloman, R.E. and Lewis, F.E. 1978 The 'clan': case study of a black extended family in Chicago. in Shimkin, D. and D.A. Frate eds. The Extended Family in Black Societies. pp. 201–238. The Hague: Mouton.

Holt, Grace. 1975. Metaphor, black discourse style, and cultural reality. in R.L. Williams ed., Ebonics, the True Language of Black Folks. pp. 86–95. St. Louis: Institute of Black Studies.

Hooks, Bell. 1981. Ain't I A Woman: Black Women and Feminism. Boston: South End Press.

Humphreys, Laud. 1970. Tearoom Trade. Chicago: Aldine.

Imani, Nikitah Okembe-RA. 1993. On the difference between revolutionary service and community service in Nikitah Okembe-RA Imani and David Padgett eds. Verbal Shotgun: Notes on Afrikan Revolutionary Theory. unpublished manuscript.

Jackson, A. M. Psychosocial aspects of the therapeutic process. in S. M. Turner and R. T. Jones (Eds.) Behavior Therapy and Black Populations: Psychosocial Issues and Empirical Findings. N.Y.: Plenum.

————. 1992. A theoretical model for the practice of psychotherapy with African populations. in African American Psychology: Theory, Research, and Practice edited by A. Burlew, W. Banks, Harriette McAdoo, and Daudi Azibo. Newbury Park: Sage.

Jackson, G. G. 1976. The African genesis of the black perspective in helping. in Professional Psychology. 7(3), 363–367.

Jackson, Nigel. Psychosocial theory vs. afrocentric perspective. Unpublished manuscript.

Jarrett, R.L. 1992a. A family case study: an examination of the underclass debate. in Gilgun J., Handel G., and K. Daley eds. Qualitative Methods in Family Research. pp. 172–197. Newbury Park, California: Sage.

————. 1992b. Community context, interfamilial processes, and social mobility outcomes: Ethnographic contributions to the study of African-American families and children in poverty. Unpublished manuscript.

————. 1993. Voices from below: the value of ethnographic research for informing public policy. Unpublished manuscript.

Jeffers, C. 1967. Living Poor: A Participant Observer Study of Choices and Priorities. Ann Arbor, Michigan: Ann Arbor Publishers.

Jeffers, Lance. 1971. Afro-American literature, the conscience of man. in The Black Scholar. Jan. pp. 47–53.

Johnson, John M. 1975. Doing Field Research. New York: Free Press.

Jones, A. C. 1980. A conceptual model for treatment of black patients. Personal correspondence.

Jones, Reginald. 1980. Black Psychology. 2nd ed. N.Y.: Harper and Row.

Katz, P.A. and Taylor, D.A. (Eds.) 1988. Eliminating Racism: Profiles in Controversy. Plenum Publishing: N.Y.

King, Mae. 1973. The Politics of Sexual Stereotypes in Black Scholar. Vol. 4, Nos. 6 and 7, 12–23. San Francisco: Black World Foundation.

Klockars, Carl B. 1977. Field ethics for the life history. in Robert Weppner. ed. Street Ethnography. pp. 201–26. Beverly Hills, Calif.: Sage.

————. 1979. Dirty hands and deviant subjects. in Carl B. Klockars and Finnbarr W. O'Connor. eds. Deviance and Decency. pp. 261–82. Beverly Hills, Calif.: Sage.

Knapp, M.S. 1985. Ethnographic contributions to evaluation research: the experimental schools program evaluation and some alternatives. in Cook, T.D. and C.S. Reichardt eds. Qualitative and Quantitative Methods in Evaluation Research. pp. 118–139. Beverly Hills, California: Sage.

Kotarba, Joseph A. and Andrea Fontana, eds. 1984. The Existential Self in Society. Chicago: University of Chicago Press.

Lacey, C. 1970. Hightown Grammar. Manchester: Manchester University Press.

Ladner, J. A. 1971 Tomorrow's Tomorrow: The Black Woman. New York: Anchor Books.

Lasch, Christopher. 1979. The Culture of Narcissism: American Life in an Age of Diminishing Expectations. N.Y.: W. W. Norton & Co.

Leonard, P. and Jones, A. C. Theoretical consideration for psychotherapy with black clients. in R. C. Jones (Ed.) Black Psychology. 2nd ed. N.Y.: Harper and Row.

Levy, Steven. 1984. Hackers: Heroes of the Computer Revolution. N.Y.: Bantam.

Liebow, E. 1967 Tally's Corner: A Study of Negro Streetcorner Men. Boston: Little Brown.

Lockhart, L., P.D. Kurtz, R. Sutphen, K. Gauger. 1990. [Southern state's] Juvenile Justice System: A Retrospective Study of Racial Disparity. Research report to the [Southern state] Children and Youth Coordinating Council.

Mannheim, K. 1971. On the interpretation of Weltanschauung. in K. Wolff. ed. From Karl Mannheim pp. 8–58. New York: Oxford University Press.

Mannoni, O. 1960. Appel de la federation de France du FLN. in El Maudjahid. Vol. 59. pp. 644–645.

Martin, E. and Martin, J.M. 1978. The Black Extended Family. Chicago: University of Chicago Press.

Maslow, A.H. 1954. Motivation and personality. Harper and Row: N.Y.

Mbiti, J. 1970. African Religions and Philosophy. Garden City, New Jersey: Anchor Books (Doubleday).

Memmi, Alfred. 1965. The Colonizers and the Colonized. Boston: Beacon Press.

Miller, S. M. 1952. The participant observer and "over-rapport" in American Sociological Review. Vol. 5 (6), pp. 97–9.

Nobles, Wade. 1976. Black people in white insanity: an issue for community mental health. in Journal of Afro-American Issues. #4,1 Winter. pp. 21–27.

———. 1976. Extended self: rethinking the so-called negro self-concept. in The Journal of Black Psychology. 2(2), 15–24.

———. 1977. The rhythmic impulse: the issue of africanity in black family dynamics. Paper presented to the 2nd Annual Symposium on Black Psychology, Black Students Psychology Association, and Department of Psychology, Ann Arbor, Michigan.

———. 1980. African philosophy foundations for Black psychology. in Black Psychology. edited by R. Jones. 2nd ed. New York: Harper and Row.

Neal, Larry. 1972. The ethos of the blues. in The Black Scholar. Summer. pp. 42–48.

Ogbu, J. 1974. The Next Generation: An Ethnography of Education in an Urban Neighborhood. New York: Academic Press.

O'Hanlon W.H. and M. Weiner-Davis. 1989. In search of solutions: New directions in psychotherapy. New York: Norton.

Paul, B.D. 1953 Interviewing techniques and field relations. In A.C. Kroeber (ed.) Anthropology Today: An Encyclopaedic Inventory. Univ. of Chi. Press.: Chicago, Illinois.

Pedersen, P. 1988. A Handbook for Developing Multicultural Awareness. American Association for Counseling and Development: Alexandria, Va.

Peristiany, J. 1966. Honor and Shame. Chicago: University of Chicago Press.

Pitt-Rivers, Julian. Honour and social status. in J. Peristiany. ed. Honour and Shame. pp. 19–78. Chicago: University of Chicago Press.

Powdermaker, H. 1966. Stranger and Friend: The Way of an Anthropologist. N.Y.: Norton.

Rainwater, L. 1970. Behind Ghetto Walls: Black Families in a Federal Slum. Chicago: Aldine Publishing Company.

Rappaport, J. 1977. Community psychology: Values, research, and action. Holt, Rinehart, and Winston.

Redmond, Eugene. 1971. The black American epic: its roots, its writers. in The Black Scholar. Jan. pp. 15–22.

Reed, A. Junior. 1988 The liberal technocrat. in The Nation. No. 246 February 6. pp. 167–170. New York: The Nation Company.

Rist, R. 1973. The Urban School: A Factory for Failure. Cambridge, Massachusetts: Massachusetts Institute of Technology Press.

Rochford, E. Burke Jr. 1985. Hare Krishna in America. New Brunswick, N.J.: Rutgers University Press.

Rosenfeld, G. 1971. Shut Those Thick Lips: A Study of Slum School Failure. New York: Holt, Rinehart, and Winston.

Sabshin, Melvin, Diesenhaus, H. and Waxenberg, B. 1970. Dimensions of institutional racism in psychiatry. in American Journal of Psychiatry. 119, pp. 456–460.

Sanchez, G.I. 1932. Group differences and Spanish-speaking children- a critical review. in Journal of Applied Psychology. Vol. 16. pp.549–558.

Scheff, T. 1968. Negotiating reality: notes on power in the assessment of responsibility. in Social Problems 16(1), pp. 3–17.

Schiele, J.H. 1996. Afrocentricity: an emerging paradigm in social work practice. In Social Work. Vol. 14 no. 3, pp. 284–294.

Selekmen, Matthew. 1991. The solution-oriented parenting group: a treatment alternative that works. in Journal of Strategic and Systemic Therapies. Vol. 10. No. 1. pp. 36–49.

Silverstein, B. and R. Krate. 1975. Children of the Dark Ghetto: A Developmental Psychology. New York: Praeger.

Simmel, Georg. 1955. The Web of Group Affiliations. Glencoe, Illinois: Free Press.

Smilkstein, Gabriel, Toni Shaffer, Gloria Kodzwa, and James Howard. 1978. The value of health screening in medical education. in Journal of Medical Education. Vol. 53. No. 9. September. Washington, D.C.: Association of American Medical Colleges.

Smith, Dorothy. 1993. The standard north American family in The Journal of Family Issues. Vol. 14. No. 1. March, pp. 50–65. Dayton, Ohio: Sage.

Smitherman, Geneva. 1977. Talkin and Testifyin. Boston: Houghton Mifflin.

Sobel, Mechal. 1979. Trabelin' On: The Slave Journey to an Afro-Baptist Faith. Princeton: Princeton University Press.

Stack, Carol D. 1974. All Our Kin: Strategies for Survival in a Black Community. New York: Harper and Row.

Sullivan, M. 1985. Teen Fathers in the Inner City. New York: Ford Foundation.

Toldson, I. C. and Pasteur, A. B. 1975. Developmental stages of black self-discovery: implications for using black art forms in group interaction. in Journal of Negro Education. 44(2), 130–138.

Turner, R. H. 1962. Role-taking: process versus conformity. in A. M. Rose (ed.) Human Behaviour and Social Processes. London: Routledge and Kegan Paul.

Valentine, B.L. 1978. Hustling and other Hard Work: Life Styles of the Ghetto. New York: Free Press.

Vontress, C.E. 1971. Counseling Negroes. N.Y.: Houghton Mifflin.

Webber, Thomas L. 1978. Deep Like The Rivers. New York: W.W.Norton.

Welsing, Frances Cress 1991. The Isis Papers: Keys to the Colors. Chicago: Third World Press, preface.

White, Joseph. 1970. Toward a black psychology. in Ebony. Sept., pp. 44–45, 48–50, 52.

———. 1984. The Psychology of Blacks: An Afro-American Perspective. Englewood Cliffs, N.J.: Prentice-Hall.

White, M. and D. Epston. 1990. Narrative means to therapeutic ends. New York: Norton.

Whyte, William F. 1955. Street Corner Society. Chicago: University of Chicago Press.

Williams, M. On The Street Where I Lived. New York: Holt, Rinehart, and Winston Press.

Wilson, Reginald. "The historical concept of pluralism and the psychology of black behavior. pp. 41–56.

Wilson, William Julius. 1987. The Truly Disadvantaged: The Inner City, Underclass, and Public Policy. Chicago: University of Chicago Press.

Woolley, Benjamin. 1992. Virtual Worlds: A Journey in Hype and Hyperreality. Blackwell Publishers: Cambridge, Massachusetts.

Yankelovich, D. and Barrett, W. 1970. Ego and instinct: The psychoanalytic vein of human nature. N.Y.: Random House.

Zollar, A.C. 1985. A Member of the Family: Strategies for Black Family Continuity. Chicago: Nelson-Hall.

Index

About the Author

Dr. Nikitah Okembe-RA Imani serves as associate professor of sociology and Africana Studies at James Madison University. He received his BSFS degree in international politics specializing in International Relations Law and Organization from Georgetown University (1989). He subsequently earned a master's degree in political science (1991), a master's degree in sociology (1992), and a Ph.D. in sociology from the University of Florida (1995). Dr. Imani was the co-author of *The Agony of Education*, a study of the experience of African students at predominantly Euro-American colleges and universities (Routledge, 1996). Dr. Imani is the son of Mr. and Mrs. Eulas C. Strong and has a son, Kamau Okembe-RA Imani and a daughter Kandyce Brene L'Joy Bartee.

Breinigsville, PA USA
15 December 2010
251520BV00003B/5/P